Your TFSA Compounder

Work Your TFSA Harder
So You Can Retire Sooner

Henry Mah, CMA

"Compound interest is the eighth wonder of the world. He who understands it, earns it ... he who doesn't ... pays it."

-Albert Einstein

Your TFSA "Compounder" will show you how to achieve financial independence by putting the money you save in a Tax Free Savings Account (TFSA) and then investing those funds with the Income investment strategy.

These alone are just a savings account and an investment strategy. Together, they are so much more.

Henry Mah, CMA

Disclaimer

The information and opinions in this book must not be considered investment advice. The information is intended to be for informational purposes only. I am not an investment advisor and I am not recommending any security or investment product. Nor do I receive any compensation for suggesting website links or sources to find any data suggested in the book.

Opinions offered here can never be a substitution for independent analysis and due diligence. The book may contain some forward-looking statements and opinions on subject matter that is familiar and already well-covered. Your guess as to the future value of any security is as good as mine, or that of a broker. Forecasting is an unreliable enterprise.

There are always risks involved with investing and investors must expect occasional losses on the risk they take. It is certain there will be periods of time when all investing strategies, including dividend growth investing, will underperform the market. It is always best to have measured expectations when approaching investing in any form.

I dedicate this book to my lifelong partner, friend and always my inspiration, Raelene.

Special thanks to my daughter Theresa for editing the book and my grandson Sam for doing the cover artwork.

Table of Contents

Foreword

As a passionate do-it-yourself investor for many years now, I've tried to learn from my investing experiences - both the good and the not-so-good. And for good reason. I believe those that fail to learn from their mistakes are likely doomed to repeat them.

But major financial mistakes need not apply to you. Not by a long shot. In fact, that is where this book, *Your TFSA Compounder*, can help. You can learn from others.

One lesson I learned that I continually try and pay forward using my blog, was actually a gift to all adult Canadian investors: the Tax Free Savings Account (TFSA).

The TFSA was first introduced in our 2008 Canadian federal budget by then Finance Minister Jim Flaherty. Thankfully, the account became effective to contribute to soon after, at the very start of the 2009 calendar year. While the initial TFSA contribution dollar limit of $5,000 was initially scoffed at by some (too low to create any meaningful wealth), I personally believed from day 1 the TFSA could potentially transform my financial well-being over time.

And it has.

When Henry honored me to share this Foreword with you, I reflected upon my financial journey to date and the lessons learned shared on my blog. After failing to grow my portfolio using high-priced mutual funds and chasing penny stocks, I learned that money that makes money, can make more money. And money that makes more money, is even better, *when it's tax free*. That's exactly what the TFSA can deliver.

Since taking lessons learned to heart and realizing the TFSA could be a dream-like tax-free investing account (not as a "savings" account based on the poorly branded name), I've managed to invest in a way that delivers some healthy and growing income. And you can too. What started out for me as an initial $5,000 contribution to the TFSA, that money has grown over time into a six-figure portfolio. This occurred because of diligent yearly TFSA contributions and investing in assets that pay dividends and grow them over time. Such investments inside the TFSA, that you'll learn how to select in *Your TFSA Compounder*, now churn out almost $5,000 per year in passive, tax-free income.

For those of you striving to beat the market or get-rich quickly, this book is not for you. For those of you striving to invest in a way that delivers meaningful, growing, tax-free income with time, I suggest you keep reading.

Like Henry, I've learned to embrace the TFSA as an investment account. In doing so, it has put me on an incredible path of financial prosperity.

I hope by reading *Your TFSA Compounder* you can make up your own mind about how to leverage the power of the TFSA - and be wealthier for it.

Happy investing!

Mark Seed
DIY Investor
Creator and owner of *My Own Advisor* blog
www.myownadvisor.ca

Preface

Before we get started, I'd like you to remember a few things as you read through this book:

1. This book is not going to tell you how to get rich quick, or how to make a fast million from your TFSA. Trust me, I want to help you achieve financial security, and we will! Just slowly and steadily.
2. Starting to save sooner rather than later is always best, but if you're a late starter, it does not mean you cannot still achieve your retirement goal.
3. The term "income" almost always refers to fixed income products like GICs, bonds, or other fixed assets. When I refer to income in this book, I'll mean how much income your stocks will generate.
4. You won't find any projections on how your capital investments will grow (which is how everyone else estimates TFSA growth). Market value is not my focus, instead I'll show you how the income from your investments will grow.
5. I can suggest a path and process to follow to achieve your retirement goal, but the bulk of the work, making it happen, will be up to you.
6. Some of the numbers used in my examples and charts may not reflect current figures when you read the book, but the points I'm trying to make are still valid.
7. I apologize for some of the fuzzy charts, they lose their resolution when condensed in size.
8. Much of the stock evaluation information will detail a step-by-step process like a workbook or exercise book. It might seem like back-to-school time, but what you'll learn could well make all the difference to your future.
9. By following my strategy, the income from your TFSA should meet your future expenses and be totally tax-free.
10. Tax-free is not a phrase or word that normally applies to anything in real life. Everyone remembers that famous quote of Benjamin Franklin: "but in this world

nothing can be said to be certain, except **death and taxes**".

11. You may also find that you can avoid two pitfalls you might have thought inevitable: the real possibility of outliving your finances, and the income from your investments not meeting your future needs.
12. I'll provide you with Excel worksheets so you can update and see your progress as your TFSA portfolio income grows. You'll always know how you are doing and if your efforts are on track to achieving your goal.
13. I'll try to avoid recommending individual stocks for your TFSA and other investments, instead I'll put you to the task of evaluating stocks. This book provides a set of guidelines, showing you how to gather the data, how to analyze the data (as best I can) and then allows you to decide whether a stock qualifies.

Now, onwards and upwards, as they say!

Introduction
CRA TFSA Retirement Plan

I'm sure you may already be aware of the Canadian Tax Free Savings Account (TFSA) and have read about the advantages of having such an account. It's a great way to save for future expenses and even to fund part of your retirement. But I have learned through research and experience something you might not have seen or grasped; just how easy it can be to use a TFSA to establish a tax-free income compounder. The definition of *"Compounder"* is to earn interest on the accrued interest as well as the principal to generate more interest. With this simple yet very powerful concept you can work towards a retirement that will not require you to sell portions of your investment, will not be affected by stock market fluctuations or the continuous changes in stock prices in order for your income to grow, even after you begin withdrawing funds.

Before we go into the details of exactly what to do and how, here's some of the things you should know about a Tax-Free Savings Account, taken directly from the Canada Revenue Agency.

What is a Tax Free Savings Account (TFSA)?

Excerpted from the CRA website:

What is a TFSA?

The TFSA program began in 2009. It is a way for individuals who are 18 years of age or older and who have a valid social insurance number (SIN) to set money aside tax free throughout their lifetime.

Contributions to a TFSA are not deductible for income tax purposes. Any amount contributed as well as any income earned in the account (for example, investment income and capital gains) is generally tax-free, even when it is withdrawn.

Administrative or other fees in relation to a TFSA and any interest on money borrowed to contribute to a TFSA are not tax-deductible.

Who can open a TFSA?

Any individual who is 18 years of age or older and who has a valid SIN is eligible to open a TFSA. You cannot open a TFSA or contribute to one until you turn 18. However, when you turn 18, you will be able to contribute up to the full TFSA dollar limit for that year.

How to open a TFSA

You can have more than one TFSA at any given time, but the total amount you contribute to all your TFSAs cannot be more than your available TFSA contribution room for that year.

To open a TFSA, you must do the following:

Contact your financial institution, credit union, or insurance company (issuer); and

Provide the issuer with your SIN and date of birth so the issuer can register your qualifying arrangement as a TFSA. Your issuer may ask for supporting documents.

Self-directed TFSA

You can set up a self-directed TFSA if you prefer to build and manage your own investment portfolio by buying and selling different types of investments.

Contributions

The maximum amount that you can contribute to your TFSA is limited by your TFSA **contribution room**.

All TFSA contributions made during the year, including the replacement or re-contribution of withdrawals made from a TFSA, will count against your contribution room. Here are the allowable annual contributions from 2009 to 2020.

Year	Annual Contribution	Cumulative Contribution
2009	$5,000.00	$5,000.00
2010	$5,000.00	$10,000.00
2011	$5,000.00	$15,000.00
2012	$5,000.00	$20,000.00
2013	$5,500.00	$25,500.00
2014	$10,000.00	$35,500.00
2015	$5,500.00	$41,000.00
2016	$5,500.00	$46,500.00
2017	$5,500.00	$52,000.00
2018	$5,500.00	$57,500.00
2019	$6,000.00	$63,500.00
2020	$6,000.00	$69,500.00

At any time in the year, if you contribute more than your allowable TFSA contribution room, you will be considered to be over-contributing to your TFSA and you will be subject to a tax equal to 1% of the highest excess TFSA amount in the month, for each month that the excess amount remains in your account.

You do not need to have earned income to contribute to a TFSA.

As the account holder you are the only person who can do the following with your TFSA:

- make contributions
- make withdrawals
- determine how funds are invested

You can give your spouse or common-law partner money to contribute to their own TFSA without having that amount, or any earnings from that amount being attributed back to you, but the total contributions you each make to your own TFSAs cannot be more than your TFSA contribution room. Contributions made to a TFSA are **not** tax-deductible.

Management fees related to a TFSA trust and paid by the holder are not considered to be contributions to the TFSA. The payment of investment counsel, transfer, or other fees by a TFSA trust will not result in a distribution (withdrawal) from the TFSA trust.

How your TFSA contribution room is determined

The TFSA contribution room is made up of the total of all of the following:

- your TFSA dollar limit
- any unused TFSA contribution room from previous years
- any withdrawals made from the TFSA in the previous year

Types of permitted investments

Generally, the types of investments that are permitted in a TFSA are the same as those permitted in a registered retirement savings plan (RRSP). These would include:

- cash
- mutual funds
- securities listed on a designated stock exchange
- guaranteed investment certificates
- bonds
- certain shares of small business corporations

Losses incurred within a TFSA investment

Depending on the type of investment held in your TFSA, you may incur a loss in your original investment. Any investment losses within a TFSA are **not** considered a withdrawal and therefore are **not** part of your TFSA contribution room.

Foreign funds

You can contribute foreign funds to a TFSA. However, your issuer will convert the funds to Canadian dollars (using the exchange rate on the date of the transaction), when reporting this information to us. The total amount of your contribution, in Canadian dollars, **cannot exceed** your TFSA contribution room.

If dividend income from a foreign country is paid to a TFSA, the dividend income could be subject to foreign withholding tax.

"In kind" contributions

You can also make "in kind" contributions (for example, securities you hold in a non-registered account) to your TFSA, as long as the property is a qualified investment.

You will be considered to have disposed of the property at its fair market value (FMV) at the time of the contribution. If the FMV is more than the cost of the property, you will have to report the capital gain on your income tax and benefit return. However, if the cost of the property is more than its FMV, you cannot claim the resulting capital loss. The amount of the contribution to your TFSA will be equal to the FMV of the property.

Transfers from your RRSP

If you transfer an investment from your RRSP to your TFSA, you will be considered to have withdrawn the investment from the RRSP at its FMV, and that amount will be reported as an RRSP withdrawal, and must be included in your income in that year. The tax withheld on the withdrawal can be claimed at line 437 of your income tax and benefit return. If the transfer into your TFSA takes place immediately, the same value will be used as the amount of the contribution to the TFSA. If the contribution to the TFSA is deferred, the amount of the contribution will be the FMV of the investment at the time of that contribution.

Except in certain circumstances, you cannot exchange securities for cash, or other securities of equal value, between your accounts, either between two registered accounts or between a registered and a non-registered account (swap).

Withdrawals from a TFSA

A qualifying transfer from one TFSA to another is not considered to be a withdrawal.

Making withdrawals

Depending on the type of investment held in your TFSA, you can generally withdraw any amount from the TFSA at any time. **Withdrawing funds from your TFSA does not reduce the total amount of contributions you have already made for the year.**

Withdrawals, excluding qualifying transfers and specified distributions, made from your TFSA in the year will only be added back to your TFSA contribution room at the beginning of the following year.

Replacing withdrawals

If you decide to replace or re-contribute all or a portion of your withdrawals into your TFSA **in the same year**, you can only do so if you have available TFSA contribution room. If you re-contribute but do not have contribution room, you will have over-contributed to your TFSA in the year. You will be subject to a tax equal to 1% of the highest excess TFSA amount in the month, for each month that the excess amount remains in your account.

Death of a TFSA holder

After the holder of a TFSA dies, possible tax implications may vary depending on one or more of the following factors:

- the type of TFSA
- the type of beneficiary(ies)
- whether any income was earned after the date of death
- how long, after the date of death, before amounts are distributed to beneficiaries

Depending on the factors that apply, the following can be affected:

- whether the deceased's TFSA continues to exist or is considered to have ceased
- how income earned after the date of death may be reported and taxed
- whether a beneficiary can contribute amounts received to their own TFSA, within certain limits, and whether such a contribution would affect their unused TFSA contribution room

Types of beneficiaries

The types of beneficiaries for TFSA purposes are:

- a survivor who has been designated as a successor holder
- designated beneficiaries (for example, a survivor who has not been named as a successor holder), former spouses or common-law partners, children, and qualified donees

Determining the type of beneficiary is an important initial step and can be affected by:

- designations which may have been made in the deceased holder's TFSA contract
- the provisions of the deceased holder's will, if there is one
- provincial or territorial succession legislation

For the complete official Canada Revenue Agency guidelines for the TFSA, go to:https://www.canada.ca/en/revenue-agency/services/forms-publications/publications/rc4466/tax-free-savings-account-tfsa-guide-individuals.html

Chapter 1

No plan will work on its own

"Plans are only good intentions unless they immediately degenerate into hard work."

– Peter Drucker

"The survey of 2,047 Canadians found 53 per cent had little disposable income and that debt is overwhelming for a quarter of respondents. An increasing number – 57 per cent versus 53 per cent last year – are carrying credit card debt, the survey showed. A third of people can't afford to pay off their credit card balances while 40 per cent owe non-mortgage sums of more than $20,000..."

- *Financial Post* September 30, 2019

This entire book is a plan or guide to move you towards a successful and secure retirement. But having a plan is one thing, **turning that plan into a reality is the real work**.

I want you to plan and work towards financial freedom, but before starting on that journey one must first have their own house in order. I suggest you start by assessing your current situation:

1. Are you living within your means? Is your current income sufficient to cover your expenses?
2. Is your current debt manageable, meaning are you paying down your debt faster than it is growing?
3. Can you afford to pay your monthly credit card balance without incurring interest charges?
4. Are you willing to make the commitment needed to reduce any debts you might have and

possibly change your lifestyle to make it happen?

If your answer is No to the first three questions, but you can answer Yes to number four, don't fret. You may be ready to deal with your debt issues, which for many Canadians can be daunting. I believe the first step to getting your house in order is to outline a plan of action, at least in the short term. Make up a checklist of things or actions you can do to help address your debt. Your list should include ways to curb your spending as well as how to redirect your income to meet some of those debts. Tackle the most simple or immediate items of concern. As each item is cleared off your list, expand or revise the list to deal with more pressing debt problems and decide how you'll begin to get them under control. I believe having the right attitude about money and where it serves you best is essential. Only then can one really begin to plan and save for their retirement.

I recognize that for some it may take a real change in lifestyle, but if you are in a serious debt situation, than reducing and becoming debt-free must be your initial objective. Face your problem, acknowledge it and if necessary, seek assistance. Check out local and national credit counselling agencies, such as the Credit Counselling Society:

https://www.nomoredebts.org/canada/credit-counselling.html

The longer one delays the worse the problem will become, but if you are willing to make the commitment, anything is possible, most of all a secure retirement. The key is to reduce debt and begin saving as early as possible and keep saving. You don't need to "do without" or give up living a fulfilling lifestyle, just keep everything in perspective. Decide what's important and what goals you want for yourself and your family, both now and in the future.

Of course when I talk of future plans, let's remember that if you are married or have a family, their input and acceptance of any plan must be included.

My friend Mark Seed, of the blog, *"My Own Advisor"* (https://www.myownadvisor.ca/), is a good example of someone who recognized early on that he wanted a change of direction in his future.

If you're interested in seeing how Mark came about discovering and planning for a different retirement future, visit the following link: https://www.myownadvisor.ca/2019-financial-goals-july-update/

Another good article, is written by Michele Cagan, CPA and provides some good information on how to address a debt problem:

https://michelecagancpa.com/blog/take-control-of-your-debt/

Remember *compounding* works for or against you. If you allow debt to control your life, others are the beneficiaries. Financial independence will only happen if you take control, if you are willing to contribute towards achieving your goal, not just with money, but with time and the commitment to make it work. It is then that the *TFSA "Compounder"* can help you.

Here are 8 key findings from the study on TFSAs

1. *The number of people using TFSAs is climbing, from 56% of Canadians last year to 69% to 2018.*
2. *The total amount Canadians hold in TFSAs is up 21 percent over the past two years. Canadians hold an average of $27,053 in their TFSA this year, up from $22,008 in 2017 and $17,382 in 2016.*
3. *Contributions are down slightly from 2017, with the average contribution dropping 3.3% to $4,826 this year.*
4. *About 33 percent of Canadians are not aware of the maximum contribution amount.*
5. *Only 11 percent knew the contribution limit was going up to $6,000 annually starting in 2019. And a huge percentage of respondents—66%—didn't know that there was a change.*
6. *Taxes aren't top of mind. Fully 40% of respondents didn't know there was a tax penalty for over-contribution, up six percentage points from last year.*
7. *Half of Canadians say they will use the money for retirement and 39% plan to use it as an emergency fund.*
8. *Regionally, Canadians in B.C. and Alberta were more likely to cite not having enough money (66 percent and 54 percent respectively) as the top reason for not reaching the contribution limit.*

The bottom line? While there are economic challenges in the Western provinces especially that are making it harder for Canadians to put money aside, it's worth considering a "set-it-and-forget it" pre-authorized savings plan for your TFSA, where you contribute a set amount every month to the plan—an effortless way to save without having to think about it.

"There is an opportunity for Canadian savers to better understand this account and make sure that they are getting the most out of it".

-Matthew Lepine, BMO Financial Group, December 2018

I agree wholeheartedly with the BMO assessment. The TFSA is an untapped resource for Canadians to enjoy a tax-free secure retirement. I believe there is a lack of understanding as to exactly what a TFSA is and how or what the TFSA can be used for. Most are overlooking the real benefit of adopting it for retirement instead of as a short-term savings vehicle.

The missing components are information, understanding and then a sound user-friendly investing method to put that new-found knowledge to good use!

Who will benefit the most from this book?

1. Those who wish to manage their own self-directed TFSA.
2. Those who are just starting to invest and undecided whether to invest in an RRSP or TFSA.
3. Those who assume that a TFSA is basically a short-term savings account.
4. Those who have directed most of their investments towards an RRSP, but are still in early to middle age.
5. Those who have not invested their maximum allowed amount into their TFSA.
6. Those who are looking to maximize their TFSA in order to provide them with the most benefits in retirement, but are not sure how to achieve it or what to invest in.

Is it better to invest in an RRSP or TFSA?

Comparison between RRSP and TFSA		
	RRSP	**TFSA**
Age limit for making contributions	No	Yes
Need earned income to contribute	Yes	No
Tax-deductable contributions	Yes	No
Tax-free withdrawals	No	Yes

The most important and under-appreciated difference between a TFSA and an RRSP is that an RRSP is a tax-deferred investment, not a tax-free option.

There is a general assumption that a TFSA has little benefit for high earners as an investment tool because of the lower annual contribution cap. The TFSA is looked at commonly as a savings account for the short-term, to help accumulate funds for things like vehicles, houses or other special purchases. I believe nothing could be further from the truth.

Everyone recognizes that starting to save earlier is best no matter what account vehicle you choose. But I believe an early start makes a TFSA imperative as your first choice, primarily because of its tax-free status. Coupling this with an investment strategy that takes advantage of the power of compounding will make your savings goal that much more attainable.

I'm of the opinion one should maximize their TFSA before contributing to an RRSP, regardless of your age, and here's why:

1. Investing in a TFSA means that any income and growth from those investments will not be subject to

taxes upon withdrawal, as it is with all other savings accounts.

2. If you currently have any funds to contribute to an RRSP and still have an un-contributed balance with your TFSA, you are missing out on a powerful investing opportunity. Time-in is very important with compounding. The longer your money is invested in a tax-free account, the more benefit you get.

3. One must never forget that funds contributed to an RRSP and any growth on those investments are going to be taxed upon withdrawal. You are just delaying the taxes to be paid on those investments.

4. Investing in a TFSA (maximizing your contribution) might mean less initial tax savings, but I believe the risk of higher taxes later through an RRSP or RRIF is a greater penalty.

5. The more your RRSP grows the higher your tax rate becomes. No matter how big your TFSA gets it remains tax-free.

6. For those that still have un-contributed room in a TFSA and currently reinvest their RRSP tax rebate by returning those funds to an RRSP are missing a meaningful financial opportunity. It is important to remember that those funds and any growth within that RRSP will also be taxed, negating the benefit. The RRSP rebate is essentially a government loan.

7. By putting your RRSP rebate into a TFSA you won't get a current tax break but you will have access to your money without tax penalties, and all of the earnings are tax-free. Trust me, when the time comes to withdraw those funds, that tax-free status will be very welcome!

8. If you have the opportunity to have more than one TFSA in a household (for example, a spousal TFSA) take advantage of it. It will allow you to contribute double the annual maximum and further accelerate your tax-free future income.

I am not saying one should never contribute to an RRSP. Certainly, if one has maximized their TFSA contribution than additional investments can go into an RRSP. What I am saying is that you should make the TFSA your premier retirement account before investing retirement funds in any other account. By prioritizing your TFSA contributions before allocating any additional funds to an RRSP or other investment account you will find that even a little bit goes a long way, making compounding more effective within your TFSA, which should be your ultimate goal. And remember, those funds will be tax-free, when you need it the most!

To illustrate how valuable I feel boosting your TFSA can be for those who have not contributed the maximum allowable amount, I have created a chart that maps out the maximum accumulation one is allowed by age and the year that one opens a TFSA up to 2022. The longer a person over 18 waits to open a TFSA the larger the un-contributed amount grows. The right two columns show how much one's un-contributed TFSA balance is when they turn 18 after 2009 to 2022.

Allowable TFSA maximums by age and year															
Age 18	Age 19	Age 20	Age 21	Age 22	Age 23	Age 24	Age 25	Age 26	Age 27	Age 28	Age 29	Age 30	Age 31	Max	18 As
2009	2010	2011	2012	2013	2014	2015	2016	2017	2018	2019	2020	2021	2022	2022	Of
5,000	5,000	5,000	5,000	5,000	5,000	5,000	5,000	5,000	5,000	5,000	5,000	5,000	5,000	81,500	2009
	5,000	5,000	5,000	5,000	5,000	5,000	5,000	5,000	5,000	5,000	5,000	5,000	5,000	76,500	2010
		5,000	5,000	5,000	5,000	5,000	5,000	5,000	5,000	5,000	5,000	5,000	5,000	71,500	2011
			5,000	5,000	5,000	5,000	5,000	5,000	5,000	5,000	5,000	5,000	5,000	66,500	2012
				5,500	5,500	5,500	5,500	5,500	5,500	5,500	5,500	5,500	5,500	61,500	2013
					5,500	5,500	5,500	5,500	5,500	5,500	5,500	5,500	5,500	56,000	2014
						10,000	10,000	10,000	10,000	10,000	10,000	10,000	10,000	50,500	2015
							5,500	5,500	5,500	5,500	5,500	5,500	5,500	40,500	2016
								5,500	5,500	5,500	5,500	5,500	5,500	35,000	2017
									5,500	5,500	5,500	5,500	5,500	29,500	2018
										6,000	6,000	6,000	6,000	24,000	2019
											6,000	6,000	6,000	18,000	2020
												6,000	6,000	12,000	2021
													6,000	6,000	2022
5,000	10,000	15,000	20,000	25,500	31,000	41,000	46,500	52,000	57,500	63,500	69,500	75,500	81,500		

2022 with spouse maximum	$163,000.00

Note: **I've updated this chart and part of this section to reflect the 2022 maximum allowable contribution.**

A lot of useful information can be pulled from this chart. For example:

1. If you were age 18 in 2009, the year the TFSA was introduced, but did not make any contributions at all, you would have room for $81,500.00 in your TFSA by the year 2022.
2. If you turned 18 years old after 2009, you will not have access to any previous years' TFSA contributions (see the last two columns on the right). You can only contribute the maximum amount into the TFSA for the year you turn 18 and thereafter. For example, someone turning 18 in 2015 can only contribute a maximum of $50,500 by 2022 to their TFSA.
3. It is important to remember that anytime you do not invest the maximum yearly amount, you can add those funds to your TFSA account in subsequent years. For example, if a 26-year old opens a TFSA in 2017 and adds $3,000 per year from 2017 to 2022, for a total of $18,000, they would still have $63,500 of un-contributed TFSA funds which can be added in later years. In 2022 their maximum allowable is $81,500 minus $18,000, leaving $63,500.

For anyone over the age of 18 with money to invest, I cannot stress enough that the earlier you invest in a TFSA the better. Be sure to maximize your TFSA, including any un-contributed funds, before investing in an RRSP. This will allow your TFSA funds to grow and compound at its fastest possible rate. And the most important point to remember is that the funds will be tax-free.

Now let's take a look at someone who is age 31 or older as of 2022. If their gross salary is between $35,000 and $55,000, their maximum annual RRSP contribution limit would be between $6,300 and $9,900 (18% of their earned income less any pension adjustments rules):
https://www.canada.ca/en/revenue-agency/services/tax/individuals/topics/rrsps-related-

plans/contributing-a-rrsp-prpp/contributions-affect-your-rrsp-prpp-deduction-limit.html

If they have not opened a TFSA, or have contributed less than the maximum, their total TFSA contribution limit in 2022 is $81,500, less any contributions to date.

If they can afford to invest the $6,300 to $9,900 (or a lessor amount) to an RRSP they should instead put the money into their TFSA, to reduce their un-contributed TFSA limit (the $81,500 or the balance available) as quickly as possible.

Also, if they have investments in a non-registered account and have un-contributed room in their TFSA, they might wish to consider an In-Kind transfer of the stocks into their TFSA. There may be capital gains to claim, but the goal is to get as much investment money into the TFSA as soon as possible.

After reaching the TFSA maximum, then they can begin contributing to their RRSP. I'll demonstrate later in the book that the sooner you maximize your TFSA contributions the greater your tax-free income will grow.

Remember, I am suggesting that your TFSA become your premier retirement fund and you consider the money put into the fund as untouchable until you decide to withdraw needed funds during retirement.

Take it from someone who did not have the opportunity to invest in a vehicle like the TFSA during my accumulation phase, but had to contribute large sums into an RRSP. We are paying the price now. Oh, how I wish I could have contributed five or six thousand dollars a year into a tax-free investment right from the beginning, one which does not result in our withdrawals being taxed at the highest rate.

Not only are we still in a high tax bracket in our retirement, but we are subject to an Old Age Security pension clawback. My goal is to offer people a very real solution to the "pain" of losing hard-earned savings to taxes when they need it the most, long before an emergency might derail a comfortable retirement.

It is often recommended that everyone should have savings or an emergency fund. The amount and size of those savings will vary depending upon your age, financial status, family situation and possible health issues. This is a very good idea, but remember to keep these funds separate from your TFSA. Don't interrupt the power of compounding you will have started. You do not want to jeopardize your future income by withdrawing any funds you have set aside for your retirement.

The 130% advantage to maximizing a TFSA

1. Every dollar you invest in your TFSA is worth 130% more than a dollar put into an RRSP. For example, if you invest $175,000 into your TFSA you'd have to invest at least $227,500 into an RRSP to get the same net return.
2. Every dollar of growth within a TFSA is worth 130% more than the same growth within an RRSP. If you invested the same amount and in the same manner into a TFSA and an RRSP, they should grow at the same rate. But the growth within the RRSP is lost when the funds are taken out and subjected to taxation.
3. The income withdrawn from a TFSA is worth 130% more than monies taken out of an RRSP. Again, it's the higher taxes you pay on the income and the loss in purchasing power from an RRSP withdrawal. If you withdraw $52,000 from your TFSA you'd have to take $67,600 from an RRSP to have an equivalent amount, when allowing for taxes.
4. It takes less money overall to fund your retirement if you contribute the allowable maximum into a TFSA than an RRSP. The more you invest in the *TFSA "Compounder"* strategy, the more it grows, and all of the growth is tax-free.
5. At the date of death, an RRSP/RRIF is included in the income of the deceased for the tax return for the year of death. However, income tax may be deferred if the beneficiary of the RRSP, RRIF, or estate is the spouse or common-law partner. Otherwise the full market value of the RRSP/RRIF becomes taxable income.

    2020 Canada Tax Brackets:

Over $48,535 to $97,068	20.5%
Over $97,069 to $150,472	26.0%
Over $150,473 to $214,367	29.0%
Over $214,368	33.0%

    Plus Provincial tax, which varies by Province. Your TFSA will never be taxed and distributed tax-free.

What I want to do with the concept of "the 130% advantage" is highlight the difference taxes can make upon retiring, to your savings, and ultimately to your quality of retirement. Yet, despite the advantages of the TFSA, you will find that many financial advisors still recommend the RRSP over a TFSA. Here are typical recommendations for investors:

> *"An RRSP is the go-to choice for most investors saving for retirement, and you can save on a tax-deferred basis until retirement. A TFSA can be used to save for any purpose—including retirement or short-term goals. A TFSA also lets you invest in qualified investments, tax-free, and you can contribute and withdraw funds at any time".*

> - excerpted from RBC Investing

> *"Maximizing your allowable RRSP contributions, each and every year, is generally the best investment that most Canadians can make. You get a tax deduction for the amount of your RRSP contribution, and also, because your RRSP investments compound, tax free, within the plan until you withdraw the funds. TFSAs will be popular for Canadians saving for a down payment on their first homes, or to upgrade, and also for major purchases such as autos and RVs"*

> -Straight Talk Investing

I want the TFSA to be your number one choice, then contribute any remaining savings to an RRSP, not the reverse.

If you are considering using TFSA funds to assist in buying a home, I suggest, as an alternative, the federal Home Buyer's Plan:

> *"With the federal government's Home Buyers' Plan, you can use up to $35,000 of your RRSP savings ($70,000 for a couple) to help finance your down*

*payment on a home. To qualify, the RRSP funds
you're using must be on deposit for at least 90 days.
You must also provide a signed agreement to buy or
build a qualifying home".*

*"Since the Home Buyers' Plan is considered a loan,
you must repay the amount you withdrew from your
RRSP within 15 years, with the first payment due two
years after you first withdrew the money".*

- Canadian Revenue Agency

You do have to repay the funds back into the RRSP, but
doing so over a 15 year period should not be a burden,
especially for higher income earners who can usually
maximize both their TFSA and RRSP. Check the CRA
repayment guidelines at:

https://www.canada.ca/en/revenue-
agency/services/tax/individuals/topics/rrsps-related-
plans/what-home-buyers-plan/repay-funds-withdrawn-
rrsp-s-under-home-buyers-plan.html

Let's now review the basic advantages and disadvantages of a
TFSA.

The benefits of a TFSA account

1. You can continue to contribute to a TFSA after age 71,
   which you can't with an RRSP or RRIF.
2. You can open a TFSA even if you don't have any
   earned income, unlike an RRSP.
3. All funds added to the TFSA account and any earnings
   those funds generate, by interest, dividends or capital
   gains (the value of your invested dollars increasing in
   value) will not be subject to any tax.
4. There is no tax applied to any withdrawal of funds
   from the TFSA account.

5. The TFSA can be used for any purpose. As a savings account, short-term investing, or as a long-term retirement account, which is what I recommend.
6. You are allowed to choose almost any type of investment product you wish to put in your TFSA, GICs, bonds, Preferred stocks, common stocks, mutual funds, ETFs, REITs, even foreign investments (although a withholding tax may apply).
7. Monies can be withdrawn at any time, but not replaced within the same year.
8. If you make a withdrawal, amounts withdrawn create an equal amount of contribution room that you can re-contribute the following year.

Disadvantages or Concerns with a TFSA

1. You cannot open a TFSA account until you turn 18.
2. The most common disadvantage mentioned of a TFSA is that you cannot claim the amounts contributed to reduce your taxable income. With a Registered Retirement Savings Plan (RRSP) you get to claim contributions as an income deduction, reducing your taxable income and most likely receiving a tax refund.
3. Because one does not receive a refund from their TFSA contributions, there is no opportunity to invest the refund amount and enhance compound interest.
4. Funds put into a TFSA must be after-tax dollars.
5. There is often confusion about how much one is allowed to contribute to a TFSA. The annual allowable contributions are well advertised, but how much one is allowed to make up for under-contributions from previous years is where the confusion lies.
6. Any over-contribution during a year is penalized by the Canada Revenue Agency (CRA), until the over-contribution is reduced or the maximum amount increased by CRA.

7. The annual contribution amount is often considered low, especially by high income earners.

8. There is no limit to the number of TFSA accounts one may have, but the annual and maximum contributions limits still apply across all accounts. If one has several TFSA accounts, often there is confusion or errors on the contribution limits.

9. Every time you do a transfer between multiple TFSAs, you will be eating into your annual contribution limit. You must do a "direct transfer" by having the bank or whomever holds the TFSA account do the transfer, thereby avoiding over-contributions.

10. When your investments in a TFSA make money that's a capital gain and you pay no taxes on the gain. However, when your investments lose money, even though that's a capital loss you cannot deduct the capital losses from your capital gains, which most people recognize when doing their annual tax returns.

11. You also cannot add capital losses to your future TFSA contributions. For example, if you invested the maximum contributable amount for the year, then lost any portion of that investment, you would not be allowed to add that loss to next year's maximum allowable amount. If you did, you would be penalized for over-contributing (unless you had an un-contributed TFSA balance).

12. If you invest in US or foreign stocks you will pay a withholding tax on any dividends received.

This might appear discouraging as there seems to be more disadvantages than advantages to owning a TFSA. Don't be, not only do the advantages outweigh the disadvantages, but I'll show you how easy it will be to take the money you invest in your TFSA and grow it at a rate that most don't believe is possible, you'll see!

The *TFSA "Compounder"* investment strategy we'll follow

My strategy, though basic, is two-pronged. It involves directing as much of your savings as you can afford and are allowed to towards a TFSA and investing those funds in the Income investment strategy. I believe utilizing both will allow you to achieve your retirement goal of generating sufficient income from your TFSA to retire without needing to sell capital to meet your living expenses.

The Income investment strategy was presented in my first book, *Your Ever Growing Income: The Rising Yield on Investments*. Here's a summary of the Income investment strategy taken from that book:

- Instead of concentrating on capital appreciation (price of your stocks rising), we will focus on the income your stocks generate.
- Instead of comparing your returns to market indexes or other common benchmarks, we will measure your income growth.
- Instead of worrying about being fully diversified (spreading your investments "across the board"), we will concentrate on selecting a few of the best stocks.
- Instead of providing you with a list of recommended stocks or sample portfolios, **you** will learn to evaluate the stocks, using our four-rule test and decide which best suits your needs.
- You won't be constantly looking for new stocks to buy.
- You will avoid jumping on the latest "hot" stock (like Netflix or the "cannabis craze").
- You won't be monitoring the price of your stocks, worrying when the market changes direction or be concerned should the value of your portfolio drop.
- You won't have to wait until the end of the year to see how your investment strategy is working. You will receive confirmation updates each month or quarter.

- You will, over time, learn to ignore stock prices and market fluctuations.

Have you noticed that when I refer to Income investing, there is not a mention of fixed assets, such as bonds, GICs, Preferred Shares, or any other products which only provide you with a fixed return? Fixed assets may be suitable for savings or funds set aside for unexpected expenses, but for your TFSA investments I want a growing income, not a fixed one.

Why invest for income with your *TFSA?*

- Seeking Income will make your investment choices easier,
- You will mostly invest in large, stable and profitable companies,
- You will see your income grow each month or quarter,
- Your income will not be affected by short-term market fluctuations,
- Your growing income will also grow the stock price and therefore the value of your holdings, and
- By investing in a TFSA you will see the magic of tax-free compounding at work.

Compounding happens when the money you invest pays dividends (income). Those dividends get added to your initial investment, and then they start earning dividends too. So now your dividends are continually earning more dividends.

And if you combine compounding with consistent savings, adding more money and buying more quality dividend growth stocks, your income and wealth will build that much faster. Should the company(s) raise the dividend, then all your previous investments earn even more dividends, which generates more dividends – and that's even greater compounding.

Besides the continuous increase of dividends, one of the most important components of the compounding process is time. More time means more money and greater growth. And even though other investment accounts can achieve the exact same growth if invested in the same fashion, the greatest advantage of the TFSA is that its funds will be tax-free upon withdrawal.

The Three S's of Income Investing

Simple: Income investing is one of the simplest forms of investing. By using the four-rule test (discussed later) to screen stocks you eliminate the lower quality dividend growth stocks. Evaluating a company's past performance and deciding which stocks to add to your "List of Stocks to Consider" becomes a simple process. Once you've compiled your own "List of Stocks to Consider", deciding which stocks to buy and when will be determined by the income the stocks will provide.

Sure: Income growth investing is a sure way to generate a growing income regardless of how the market reacts. By sticking with companies that have grown their earnings for long periods and regularly paid out a portion to shareholders, it makes those future payments almost a certainty. By reinvesting the dividends, you receive, you will generate income even if you stop adding funds to your portfolio.

Safe: Yes, there are risks with investing, but large, stable dividend growth companies are possibly the safest stocks one can find. As the companies pay and grow the dividend your investment becomes safer the longer you hold the stocks. That's the double dip advantage, you will receive more income over time and the value of your holdings will also rise.

Types of investment to choose for your TFSA

The TFSA regulations allow for almost any type of investments, including, but not limited to: cash, GICs, bonds, mutual funds, ETFs, REITs, and Canadian stocks. Should you invest in foreign and US stocks, a withholding tax may apply. An example of an investment which pays its dividend in US dollars and is not subject to the withholding tax are British ADRs. You can even hold and settle trades in U.S. dollars in your TFSA. You can also contribute and withdraw in U.S. dollars if you have a U.S. dollar bank account. In this case, it is the equivalent Canadian dollar value that is recorded for reporting the amounts to the CRA and you will be required to complete a W-8BEN form (certificate of foreign status of beneficial owners for US tax withholding and reporting).

I, however, recommend you stick with Canadian dividend paying companies for your *TFSA "Compounder"*. All my projections are based upon Canadian investments of income-producing dividend growth stocks which have consistently paid and raised their dividend. One can look to other investments, but I believe that you'll do just as well, in fact better, with Canadian stocks.

We'll look for companies that pay you dividends for buying and holding their shares. Then we'll further screen out the dividend payers which have not grown their dividend consistently over time, leaving you with a select group of dividend growth stocks, which will provide you with more income for each share you own, and not requiring you to sell shares to receive the higher income.

You will obtain the maximum income from holding individual stocks, not a bundle (i.e. Index Mutual Funds or Exchange Traded Funds) which will most likely include mediocre stocks. An index fund must hold all the company stocks which make up the index, which will include dividend-paying stocks, growth stocks, but also cyclical stocks, non-dividend paying stocks and even low-growth stocks. I want you to consider only those equities with at least 10 years of positive growing earnings and a history of passing along a percentage of those earnings to the shareholder. All the other stocks in an index fund will only drag down your potential income because they either don't pay you an income or the income will not grow at an acceptable rate. Remember, our main objective is income growth not just price growth.

Why not just buy an ETF?

ETFs (Exchange Traded Funds) are fast becoming the choice of many investors. They are a way to have a diversified portfolio of stocks or bonds in a single investment and can be traded just like a stock. The fees are low and they offer vast diversification, a way to "cover all the bases" if you will. Some suggest that if you own around three to five ETFs you'll cover the entire Canadian, US, Emerging and International markets. However, there are now about 22 Canadian ETF Providers and 495 ETFs available to choose from, with new ETFs coming out almost weekly. Considering that ETFs can contain hundreds, if not thousands of individual stocks, it is no longer a simple choice, is it?

For those who have set market returns as their objective ETFs may be a good choice. ETF returns generally match the market but their distributions fluctuate along with the market. Therefore, from an income perspective and for our *TFSA "Compounder"*, I do have a few objections to ETFs, mainly because:

- They hold too many stocks, the good, bad and in-between, which results in average or lower income and returns,
- The distribution (Income) fluctuates up and down with the market, rarely grows or grows at a slower rate,

- The distribution may include dividends, Return of Capital, and Capital Gains, misleading investors who assume the distribution is all dividends,
- Although ETFs' initial fees may appear to be low, the more you invest the higher the fees become,
- You have no control over the stocks chosen or their weighting within the ETF (for example, one stock may be 3.5%, while another .05% of the index),
- The fund needs to trade (constant buying and selling) to rebalance to maintain their weighting allocation,
- If you were to use our 4-Rule test (discussed later) to evaluate all the stocks in a single ETF, you would most likely find many do not meet our evaluation criteria, and
- Most ETFs try to match their performance to the market or index they represent. Since the financial crisis of 2008 the market has generally been on an upswing. But I do wonder how ETFs will do during the next major correction or extended sideways market. Personally, I do not think they will do well.

Remember, if our objective is long-term income growth for our *TFSA "Compounder"*, you will find that ETFs don't provide the consistent income growth that individual stocks can. Your money will be missing out on the opportunity for greater income growth, and that could leave you far short of your financial goals and threaten your long-term financial security.

They say when you own an ETF you own small pieces of all the companies within the fund, but I'd rather you own larger pieces of just the good dividend growth companies and not any of the others. I will be explaining further and support my hesitation to recommend ETFs with some facts when I provide my stock evaluation process.

Besides ETFs and mutual funds, the various other investment choices, such as growth or value stocks, are all dependent on price gains and the market to generate the majority of their expected returns, which is what we are attempting to avoid. I don't exclude capital growth, in fact I expect that the value of the stocks you select will grow in value in line with the dividend growth percentage. It will not be a continuous matching, but your capital will grow over time as the dividend grows. But remember that one cannot predict the future direction of the market or the price of individual stocks.

The Income investment strategy allows you to disregard the market, its continuously changing status, price fluctuation and worrying whether your holdings are performing as well as the market or index benchmarks. In fact, you will learn that market fluctuation will be a benefit to achieving your goal rather than a hindrance.

REITs for income?

I love income, but I also expect income growth. If a stock or REIT does not provide consistent income growth I don't want it. Look at these five REIT charts, not just the "Div Gth" percentage but the year-to-year change of the distributions. If the distributions decrease, are flat for extended periods or it has slow growth year-after-year look elsewhere.

HR.UN

2009	2010	2011	2012	2013	2014	2015	2016	2017	2018	Div Gth
0.720	0.789	0.975	1.176	1.355	1.469	1.243	1.358	1.380	1.380	**91.67%**

SRU.UN

2009	2010	2011	2012	2013	2014	2015	2016	2017	2018	Div Gth
1.548	1.548	1.548	1.419	1.548	1.560	1.478	1.668	1.716	1.764	**13.95%**

BEI.UN

2009	2010	2011	2012	2013	2014	2015	2016	2017	2018	Div Gth
1.800	2.300	1.800	1.720	1.950	3.435	3.040	2.238	2.256	1.992	**10.67%**

CUF.UN

2009	2010	2011	2012	2013	2014	2015	2016	2017	2018	Div Gth
1.440	1.440	1.440	1.320	1.440	1.455	1.474	1.476	1.336	1.580	**9.72%**

REI.UN

2009	2010	2011	2012	2013	2014	2015	2016	2017	2018	Div Gth
1.380	1.380	1.380	1.265	1.406	1.415	1.414	1.416	1.416	1.440	**4.35%**

Which stocks and where to find them?

I have already mentioned that I like dividend-paying stocks, and in Canada it's not too hard to find them. Still, wouldn't it be great to have a process to help us confirm their quality, especially as we are recommending that you will be holding them for many years? In addition, I do not want you to blankly accept what others may recommend as the "best" stocks to buy. **Learn to do your own evaluation and select the ones you believe are the best for you.**

The Canadian TSX Index lists about 3800 stocks and the TSX 60 Index (see Appendix A) consists of the 60 largest companies that trade on the TSX Exchange. These are the companies I want you to begin your analysis with initially: the large, profitable companies that pay dividends. Most of the stocks in the TSX 60 Index are dividend-payers, **but it is important to remember there are dividend-payers, and then there are <u>dividend-growth</u> payers.**

This is an important distinction because if a company does not raise their dividend on a regular basis than your TFSA income will not grow and compound at an accelerated rate (I'll provide an example of this later in the book). And that is the backbone of my *TFSA "Compounder"* strategy. We want to find companies which have grown their dividend on a consistent basis and for many, many years. We want to screen out the stocks which have not.

My strategy is not flashy. Nor is it about getting rich quick. The companies that you may find most suitable with my method may not be the fastest growing highest flyers, but they should provide you with a steady stream of income and, most importantly, grow that income at a reasonable and measurable rate as time goes on. This is what generates reliable income so you can ignore market fluctuation and share price.

We must consider that even the best performers' status can change over time. What were once quality dividend growth stocks 8 to 10 years ago may not qualify today. They may still be good companies which pay and grow their dividend but may not meet all the requirements to be considered good stocks **to buy** today. It's not enough to just accept what others recommend, and don't assume that all companies listed on the TSX 60 or other dividend-paying companies which have been around for a long time are the best companies to buy. Instead, I propose you put them to the four-rule test and see for yourself.

Excel worksheets

Before we start our evaluation of the TSX 60 stocks, I want to suggest, if you are not already familiar with Excel, you explore using it, or at least a similar program.

Besides providing more information than what your broker offers (from whom you purchase stocks), Excel is a very efficient method to obtain greater detail on your holdings. Excel also performs many calculations easily, such as calculating the 75% dividend growth rate, the 10-year average dividend yield of each stock, the adjusted cost base (average cost) of each stock, the annual dividend income growth, current yield and yield on your total investment percentages and growth, all of which we will discuss later.

Let's define yield

The Current Dividend Yield of any stock is the annual dividend paid by the company, divided by the current price. Since price varies hourly, daily, weekly, monthly and even yearly one might wonder why yield is important. For a dividend investor yield is similar to the interest rate of a GIC or bond. Yield tells you how much income you will receive from owning the stock if you buy it at a specific price. The higher the yield the more income you receive. We'll discuss other aspects of yield later in the book.

Back to Excel…

The TFSA template worksheets, which I have made available for download and should get you started on tracking your progress, are all created with Excel. I hope you will find Excel less daunting with these templates, especially if you are just starting with this program. I am sure that once you get started, you will find it quite intuitive.

I should point out that you will need to cross-check your data to ensure the numbers and report balances shown in Excel are correct. You should always check your Excel balances and number of shares with your broker's account balances. But even with this extra level of cross-checking, Excel will enable you to design specific reports to provide the information you wish or would like to see. I feel strongly any investment strategy benefits from diligent data tracking. Whatever method you use, I feel you will begin to look forward to tracking your progress.

You can download the "Sample Reports Cdn New and "TFSA Retire at 60" Excel packages from:
https://drive.google.com/drive/u/1/folders/1kD-ZtK7WkIINobzB3HYJ1tnwnh9P3NDf

We will now get started learning to use Excel to evaluate stocks with the "Sample Reports Cdn New" worksheet. You will initially enter the dividend data in the "TSX60" worksheet (tab at bottom) for each stock evaluated and for any added comments.

Name	Symbol	Div Cuts Yes/No	Pd Div 10Yrs Yes/No	Raised Div 10yrs Yes/No	Start Div	Ending Div	Div Gth 75% over 10yrs	Current Yield
Barrick Gold Corp	ABX						#DIV/0!	
Agnico Eagle Mines Limited	AEM						#DIV/0!	
Arc Resources Ltd	ARX						#DIV/0!	
Alimentation Couche-Tard	ATD.B						#DIV/0!	

You will also use the "%GthYld" worksheet in the "Sample Reports Cdn New" once the company has passed the four-rule test.

	2009	2010	2011	2012	2013	2014	2015	2016	2017	2018	Gth/Yld Ave
Dividend											#DIV/0!
% Chg		#DIV/0!	#DIV/0!	#DIV/0!	#DIV/0!	#DIV/0!	#DIV/0!	#DIV/0!	#DIV/0!	#DIV/0!	
Price											
Yield	#DIV/0!	#DIV/0!	#DIV/0!	#DIV/0!	#DIV/0!	#DIV/0!	#DIV/0!	#DIV/0!	#DIV/0!	#DIV/0!	#DIV/0!

We'll discuss entering the data onto the worksheets next.

So, let's get started and "sort the wheat from the chaff".

Chapter 2

Putting the stocks to the test

As I've said before, not all dividend growth stocks are created equal, and after my own successes and failures at "stock picking" I began to direct my research specifically to figure out just how to minimize risk and maximize results. If, like me, you've read other investing books, you may wonder how anyone could simplify the process of selecting and evaluating stocks. Well, you are in for a surprise, because I found it to be so simple, I wonder why everyone does not do it.

The steps are so simple that if you answer "yes" to the very first question on any stock you're researching, then you do not need to proceed further with any analysis on that stock. The stock would be immediately eliminated as a quality dividend growth (DG) stock. The other three questions can be considered guidelines and are not as fixed as the first.

The Four Guiding Rules:

1. Has the company cut their dividend in the past 10 years, yes or no?
2. Has the company paid a dividend for a minimum of 10 years (25 or more is even better)?
3. Has the company had a consistent record of raising their dividend for 10 years (the more often the increase, the better the stock)?
4. Has the dividend grown over the past 10 years by at least 75%?

The first rule is fixed because I have found that companies that cut their dividend are either a cyclical stock or it's a sign that the company has had financial problems. We want to avoid cyclical stocks because we are seeking reliable income from the companies we choose. If the company has financial problems, it will likely take many years before it recovers.

However, if a company has not cut their dividend and you answer "yes" to the other three questions, I suggest you add the company to a new list, which I like to call your "**List of Stocks to Consider**". I emphasize the word "consider" as this list needs to be flexible and monitored periodically, as it is likely to change over time. The list is intended to be your "buy" list.

Many may feel that rules are not meant to be broken, but there are valid exceptions to this four-rule test and I like to think that **if you are not flexible you risk becoming outdated**.

To illustrate my point, let's look at three different "exception" scenarios:

1. **A company has paid and raised their dividend for 10 years, but the dividend growth is less than 75%.**
   This is an example of an exception to the rules because there are companies, like utilities, that have raised their dividend for many years, I like to call them the "Steady Eddies". Many of them post a 5% dividend increase over 10 years which provides a 63% dividend growth, below our 75%, but I still consider some of them an attractive stock choice.

   One must also consider that in the event of the financial crisis and low interest rates the dividend growth rates have slowed for many companies. This kind of fluctuation should not necessarily cancel a good long-time performing stock from your list. Regardless of my example, you will have to consider the situation and decide if you wish to add the company with a lower dividend growth rate to your list.

2. **A company has only paid a dividend for 8 or 9 years (which is less than the 10-year minimum), but posts a better-than 75% growth.**

   There are examples of a company paying a dividend for less than the ideal 10-year minimum time period (by less than 10 years, I mean between 8 and 9 years. Any less would be too short a time period for serious consideration), raising their dividend yearly and posting a growth rate well above 75%. These companies might be considered new dividend growers and you may wish to give them consideration.

3. **A company has paid a dividend for 10 years, but not grown the dividend each year (perhaps, 7 of 10 years) and has a lower than 75% dividend growth rate.**

   Most Canadian banks are examples of this exception. In 2008 they were discouraged from raising their dividend until their financial reserves were higher. Beyond this development, and for many years before, their growth was steady, their dividend payout and dividend increase exceptional. My experience with Canadian bank stocks is that they are secure long-term dividend growth investments.

*Note: I am providing these "exception rules" as I don't want you to overlook a good company just because it currently does not meet all my guidelines. Still, each stock fitting into one of the three exceptions should be assessed individually, in the end it is up to you to determine your comfort level in eliminating them or not.

There has been some concern about a possible recession and should it occur it may affect some of the stocks we are considering. But remember that down markets offer Income investors the opportunity to buy shares at a lower cost and the potential to earn more income from their purchases.

So, regardless the severity of a market down-turn and the price one might be able to purchase a quality stock, you should expect that your income will not be affected even if the company does not raise their dividend, periodically. I'll explain this in more detail later in the book.

Web sources to find the data

There are several sources I will recommend to find the dividend data we'll use to evaluate stocks. Morningstar and Yahoo are my first choices, though Morningstar does have a subscription fee attached to it. You can access some of their data for free by signing up for the Morningstar "Free Access" rather than the Premium service, it is your choice. Once you've registered and logged-in you will be able to find the data needed by following the steps listed in the next section.

After discussing the Morningstar and Yahoo process, I will list two other web sources to obtain more dividend data and provide you with step-by-step procedures to enter the data into my worksheets. I think it is a good idea to use a combination of all three sources.

Note: I have no affiliation with any of the websites mentioned or receive any compensation for suggesting you use them. I have come to use these sites regularly for my own research and have found them quite useful. Feel free to use whatever sources provide you with the relevant information you need.

Using Value Line:

If you have access to your local library online, then you may also have access to Value Line. This publication will provide the dividend data for most Canadian dividend paying companies, but not all. Here is where to find the data:

1. Enter company Symbol
2. Click on PDF Reports, and current listing
3. You'll see the Div'ds per share, and the Ave yields
4. Plus other data on the company

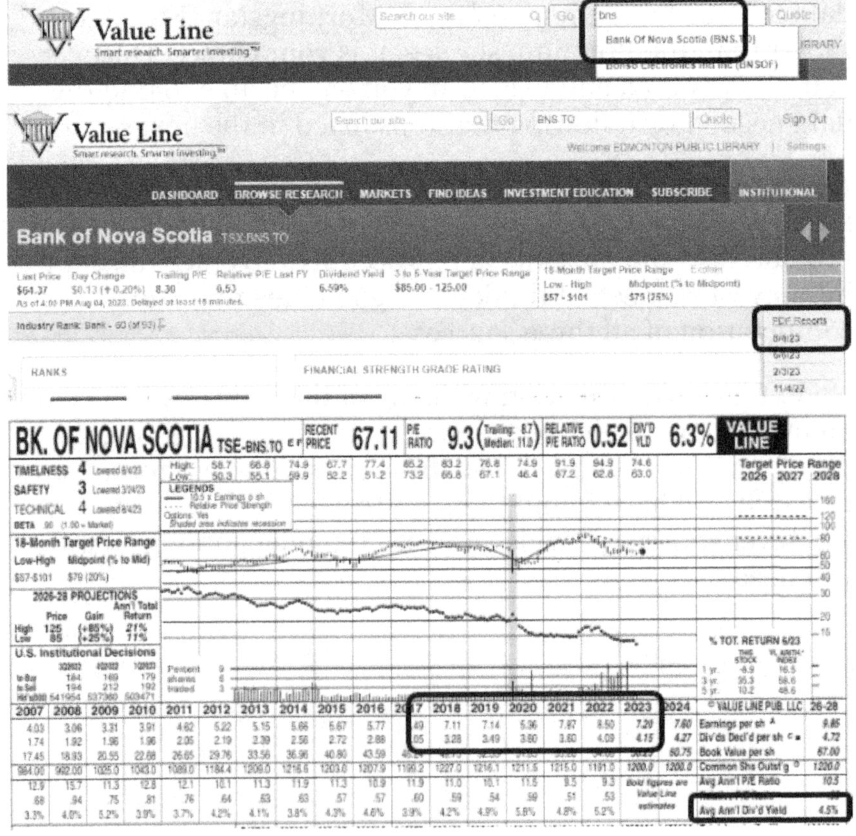

How to apply the Four Rules: Using Morningstar and Yahoo

First we will login into the Morningstar website: https://members.morningstar.ca/login.aspx#334-hidenews

Enter the stock symbol, I'll use ARX, for ARC Resources

Next click the tab: "Dividends" and arrow down to see:

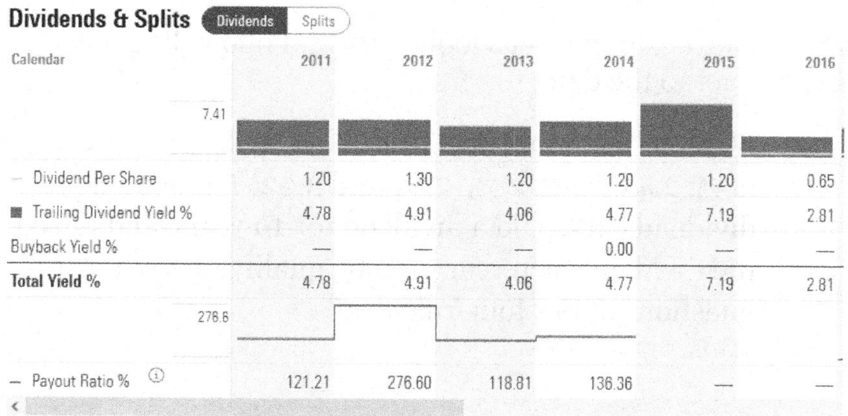

Dividends & Splits	Dividends	Splits				
Calendar	2011	2012	2013	2014	2015	2016
Dividend Per Share	1.20	1.30	1.20	1.20	1.20	0.65
Trailing Dividend Yield %	4.78	4.91	4.06	4.77	7.19	2.81
Buyback Yield %	—	—	—	0.00	—	—
Total Yield %	4.78	4.91	4.06	4.77	7.19	2.81
Payout Ratio %	121.21	276.60	118.81	136.36	—	—

You scroll to the right to see the remainder of the 10 years data:

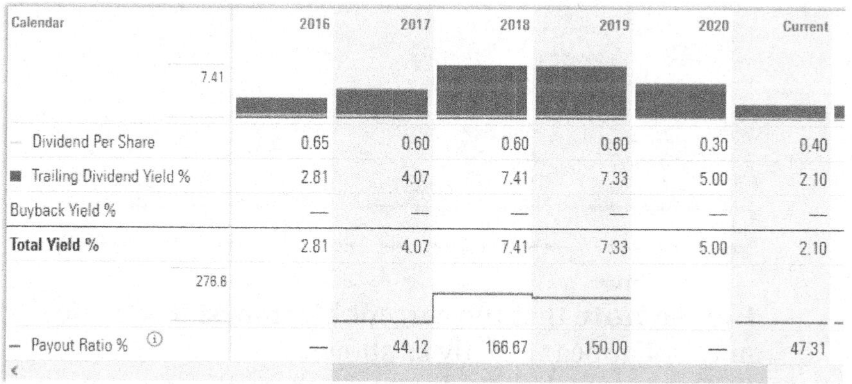

Calendar	2016	2017	2018	2019	2020	Current
Dividend Per Share	0.65	0.60	0.60	0.60	0.30	0.40
Trailing Dividend Yield %	2.81	4.07	7.41	7.33	5.00	2.10
Buyback Yield %	—	—	—	—	—	—
Total Yield %	2.81	4.07	7.41	7.33	5.00	2.10
Payout Ratio %	—	44.12	166.67	150.00	—	47.31

Record annual dividends and yields in the %Yld Gth
worksheet. The 10yr dividend Growth percentage and
Average Yield will automatically be calculated.

Just by looking at the 10-year dividends: ARX paid 1.20,
1.30, **1.20**, 1.20, 1.20, **0.70**, **0.60**, 0.60, 0.60, 0.60, **0.30**
you can see that they have cut the dividend four times (in
bold).This automatically eliminates ARX from consideration,
but record the numbers and your comments on the TSX60
worksheet.

For the next example, let's look up BCE. Follow the sames
steps to get to the data.

1. BCEs 10-year dividends were 1.58, 1.78, 2.04, 2.22,
    2.33, 2.47, 2.60, 2.73, 2.87 and 3.02. They had no
    dividend cuts, paid a dividend for 10 years, and raised
    the dividend each year thereby qualifying for 3 of 4
    questions of our four-rule test.

    BCE Inc BCE | ★★★★

	Last Price	Day Change		Open Price	Day Range	52-Week Range	Yield	Market Cap
	$56.22 ↑0.23 | 0.41%			$ 55.51	55.50-56.23	50.72-61.89	5.39%	50.5 bil

    Beta Quote Analyst Report Chart Shareholders Financials Insiders Performance **Key Stats** Valuation Filings

    Financials Export Ascending

	2008-12	2009-12	2010-12	2011-12	2012-12	2013-12	2014-12	2015-12	2016-12	2017-12
Revenue CAD Mil	17,698	17,735	18,069	19,497	19,975	20,400	21,042	21,514	21,719	22,719
Gross Margin %	71.0	74.5	72.4	39.1	48.9	48.8	48.5	48.4	49.3	49.5
Operating Income CAD Mil	3,735	3,718	3,898	3,959	4,495	4,709	4,851	5,131	5,280	5,358
Operating Margin %	21.1	21.0	21.6	20.3	22.5	23.1	23.1	23.8	24.3	23.5
Net Income CAD Mil	943	1,738	2,277	2,340	2,763	2,106	2,500	2,678	3,031	2,914
Earnings Per Share CAD	1.01	2.11	2.54	2.66	3.17	2.56	3.07	2.98	3.33	3.11
Dividends CAD	0.73	1.58	1.78	2.04	2.22	2.33	2.47	2.60	2.73	2.87
Payout Ratio %	65.2	74.3	62.5	71.4	65.5	77.4	81.9	85.0	85.3	87.8

    Source Morningstar

    Please note that the current Morningstar website
    may not appear exactly as shown.

2. BCEs 10-year dividends were 1.58, 1.78, 2.04, 2.22,
    2.33, 2.47, 2.60, 2.73, 2.87 and 3.02. They had no
    dividend cuts, have paid a dividend for 10 years and

raised the dividend each year thereby qualifying for 3 of 4 questions of our four-rule test.

3. When you enter the beginning and ending dividends on the "TSX60" worksheet the 10-year dividend growth percentage is shown. The starting dividend is 1.58 and it ends at 3.02 in 2018, to calculate its dividend growth rate use: (3.02-1.58)/1.58 x 100 = 91.14%. This shows a percentage above the 75% dividend growth rate, so BCE passes all four-rule tests and should be added to your **List of Stocks to Consider** ("Stks Consider" worksheet).

4. Because BCE passed the four-rule test, add the yearly dividend amounts onto the "%GthYld" worksheet.

BCE	2009	2010	2011	2012	2013	2014	2015	2016	2017	2018	Gth/Yld Ave
Dividend	1.58	1.78	2.04	2.22	2.33	2.47	2.60	2.73	2.87	3.02	91.14%
% Chg		12.66%	14.61%	8.82%	4.95%	6.01%	5.26%	5.00%	5.13%	5.23%	

Yld Proj | Div Gth | %Gth Yld | TSX60 | NOBL | 70 Qtr Div | 20 Mo Div | Stks Consider | NOBL Stks

5. Follow the same process to find and enter the dividend data for the remaining TSX 60 stocks and record your findings on the "TSX60" and "%GthYld" worksheets. I suggest you keep the data for all the stocks you analyze, even adding extra comments and impressions, regardless of purchase. It is very useful to track stock performances of all companies, it usually confirms, with a quick glance, why you would or would not purchase any stock.

6. I have provided a few more examples of how I applied the four-rule tests on the first eight TSX60 stocks on the chart below, this should give you a good idea of how the Excel spreadsheet works within the process.

Name	Symbol	Div Cuts Yes/No	Pd Div 10Yrs Yes/No	Raised Div 10yrs Yes/No	Start Div	Ending Div	Div Gth 75% over 10yrs	Current Yield	Consider Purchase Yes/No & Comments
Barrick Gold Corp	ABX	Yes	Yes	No	0.40	0.12	-70.00%	0.89%	No, Div Cut
Agnico Eagle Mines Limited	AEM	Yes	Yes	No	0.18	0.44	144.44%	0.87%	No, Div Cut
Arc Resources Ltd	ARX	Yes	Yes	No	1.28	0.60	-53.13%	9.22%	No, Div Cut
Alimentation Couche-Tard	ATD.B	No	Yes	Yes	0.05	0.32	540.00%	0.61%	Yes, Good Div Growth
Brookfield Asset Management	BAM.A	No	Yes	No	0.35	0.60	71.43%	1.22%	No, but maybe exception
Blackberry Limited	BB		n/a	n/a			#DIV/0!		No, no div paid
Bombardier Inc Cl. B Sv	BBD.B		n/a	n/a			#DIV/0!		No, no div paid
BCE Inc	BCE	No	Yes	Yes	1.58	3.02	91.14%	5.35%	Yes, watch payout ratio

Having you do this exercise is important because this book is not intended to provide you with a list of recommended stocks to choose from. I would rather provide you with the tools, a process by which to gather and analyze the data, so that you can come to your own conclusions and make your own decisions. Once you become comfortable with this method of evaluation, you can apply it to any stock, stocks within any index and even to an entire index itself.

I liken my four-rule test to a "Dividend Growth Sluice". It filters out the cyclical, low quality and low-growth stocks, leaving you with those few gems, the dividend growth payers!

Review the company's year-to-year dividend growth percentage change

This is the percentage change of the dividend from one year to the next.

When you enter the dividends on the "%GthYld worksheet, the dividend percentage change for each year is calculated,

BCE	2009	2010	2011	2012	2013	2014	2015	2016	2017	2018	Gth/Yld Ave
Dividend	1.58	1.78	2.04	2.22	2.33	2.47	2.60	2.73	2.87	3.02	91.14%
% Chg		12.66%	14.61%	8.82%	4.95%	6.01%	5.26%	5.00%	5.13%	5.23%	
Price											
Yield	#DIV/0!	#DIV/0!	#DIV/0!	#DIV/0!	#DIV/0!	#DIV/0!	#DIV/0!	#DIV/0!	#DIV/0!	#DIV/0!	#DIV/0!

as is the 10-year average dividend growth.

The year-to-year change in the dividend growth percentage is one of your more important evaluation measurements. We would like to see a consistent growth percentage from one year to the next, and one that does not vary too much from year to year.

When there is a sudden or extended drop in the dividend growth rate one should try to find out why. Have earnings dropped? Has the company made some large capital expenditure? Or is the company just increasing it the minimum amount to maintain its annual increases.

Should the percentage drop below 5% each year for the last three years, than this may be a sign the company is having difficulty making the dividend payment or at least maintaining the dividend growth they have in the past.

2010	2011	2012	2013	2014	2015	2016	2017	2018	2019	10 Yr Gth%
1.21	1.46	1.59	1.88	1.92	1.96	2.00	2.04	2.08	2.12	74.92%
	20.46%	9.04%	18.09%	2.13%	2.08%	2.04%	2.00%	1.96%	1.92%	

Calculating 10-Year Average Yield

The 10-year average yield is used as a guide when you wish to purchase a stock. If the current yield (the annual dividend divided by the current price) is lower than the 10-year average yield, then the stock might be considered expensive or at least on the high side. **We'd like to see the current yield to be higher than the 10-year average yield,** which would indicate the price is low and will provide you with more income than the stock has in the past.

During your analysis of the TSX60 stocks, we suggested recording the annual dividends paid, for those companies which passed the four-rule test, on the "%GthYld" worksheet. If you now enter the year-end stock price on the worksheet it will calculate the yield each year and the 10-year average

BCE	2009	2010	2011	2012	2013	2014	2015	2016	2017	2018	Gth/Yld Ave
Dividend	1.58	1.78	2.04	2.22	2.33	2.47	2.60	2.73	2.87	3.02	91.14%
% Chg		12.66%	14.61%	8.82%	4.95%	6.01%	5.26%	5.00%	5.13%	5.23%	
Price											
Yield	#DIV/0!	#DIV/0!	#DIV/0!	#DIV/0!	#DIV/0!	#DIV/0!	#DIV/0!	#DIV/0!	#DIV/0!	#DIV/0!	#DIV/0!

yield. I'll use BCE for my example:

I will obtain the price information from Yahoo Finance.

Let's go to the Yahoo website:
https://ca.finance.yahoo.com/quote/%5EGSPTSE/history/

1. **Go Yahoo finance, enter stock symbol**

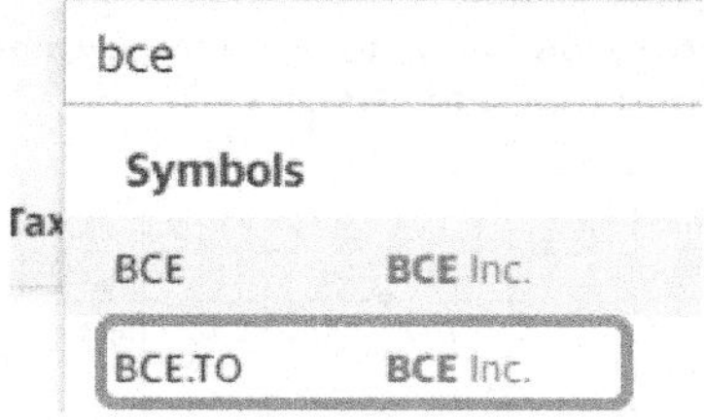

2. **Click Historical, then Enter Beginning Date, click Done**

3. **Change Frequency to Monthly, click Apply**

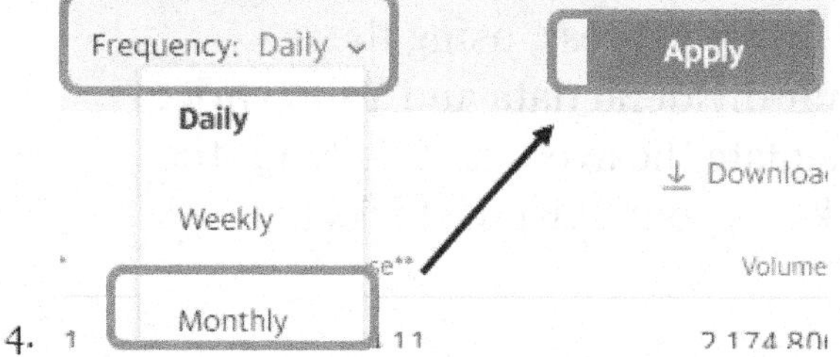

4. 1

5. **Go to the End**

6. **On the Worksheet enter 43.00, arrow key up to next January, and enter next amount (42.89). Continue for all 10 years.**

BCE	2012	2013	2014	2015	2016	2017	2018	2019	2020	2021	2022
Dividend	2.22	2.33	2.47	2.6	2.73	2.87	3.02	3.17	3.33	3.5	3.68
% Chg		4.95%	6.01%	5.26%	5.00%	5.13%	5.23%	4.97%	5.05%	5.11%	5.14%
Price	43.00	42.89									
Yield	5.16%	5.43%	#DIV/0!	#DIV/0!	#DIV/0!	#DIV/0!	#DIV/0!	#DIV/0!	#DIV/0!	#DIV/0!	

Date		Open	High	Low	Close*
Jan 01, 2013		42.89	45.10	41.75	44.31
Dec 12, 2012	**0.568** Dividend				
Jan 01, 2012		43.00	43.00	40.06	40.88
Dec 13, 2011	**0.518** Dividend				
Dec 01, 2011		39.89	42.50	39.60	42.47

When you've entered all the prices, the yield each year and the Average Yield will be calculated/

1. Follow the same process, using the Morningstar dividend data and Yahoo price data to calculate the average yield % for the other stocks on your "List of stocks to Consider".

Remember to save the worksheet as you go. I suggest you use "Save As" giving the worksheet a new name, such as "2020 Stock Analysis" or "2020-01 My Stock Worksheet".

2nd Alternative for dividend data

This next section is the 2nd Alternative source for the dividend history, The Dividend Channel. The Dividend Channel does not summarize the dividends by year, but shows when they paid the dividend, quarterly or monthly. You could add up the quarterly or monthly dividends paid and record them on the Excel worksheet or use a method of copying the monthly or quarterly dividends shown and then paste them into the appropriate Excel worksheet.

To use this method, go to the "Sample Reports Cdn New" Excel file and you will see two tabs, "70 QtrDiv" (70 Quarterly dividend-paying companies) and "20 Mo Div" (20 Monthly dividend-paying companies) worksheets which will be used to copy the dividend data for any company. This process will require a bit of computer skill and Excel knowledge. I hope the following explanation will guide you through the process.

https://drive.google.com/drive/u/1/folders/1kD-ZtK7WkIINobzB3HYJ1tnwnh9P3NDf

How to apply the Four Rules: Using the Dividend Channel

Go to The Dividend Channel online: https://www.canadastockchannel.com/

Canada Stock Channel

In the box "Enter Symbol" type the company symbol, but add .CA for any Canadian stock or fund.

Type in the first company symbol you want to evaluate in the box "Fund/Stock" at the top. I'll use ARX for ARC Resources

as my example.

Arrow down till you see the dividend history on the right side:

DIVIDEND HISTORY	
Date	**Div**[*]
06/27/19	0.050
05/30/19	0.050
04/29/19	0.050
03/28/19	0.050
02/27/19	0.050
01/30/19	0.050
12/28/18	0.050
11/29/18	0.050
10/30/18	0.050

Here comes the tricky part for some, as you will need to copy the data from the website onto your Excel worksheet.

With Excel open, click the tab "70 QtrDiv" for companies which pay quarterly dividends, or the tab "20 Mo Div" for those which pay monthly dividends. You open them by clicking the tab at the bottom of the "TSX 60" worksheet.

Quarterly Dividends		Monthly Dividends	
12/13/2018	0.755	12/28/2018	0.05
9/13/2018	0.755	11/29/2018	0.05
6/14/2018	0.755	10/30/2018	0.05
3/14/2018	0.755	9/27/2018	0.05
12/14/2017	0.718	8/30/2018	0.05
70 Qtr Div / 20 Mo Div /		70 Qtr Div / 20 Mo Div /	

Here are the steps to copy 10 years of dividend history and insert the data into the Excel worksheet:

1. We will work from the last full year of dividends, in this case it's 2018, so we will ignore the 2019 payments and start with December 28, 2018 for our example, ARX.
2. **Left Click, and Hold** the left mouse button down on the 12/28/2018.

DIVIDEND HISTORY	
Date	Div*
06/27/19	0.050
05/30/19	0.050
04/29/19	0.050
03/28/19	0.050
02/27/19	0.050
01/30/19	0.050
12/28/18	0.050
11/29/18	0.050
10/30/18	0.050
09/27/18	0.050
08/30/18	0.050

3. **Drag the mouse down** to the dividends paid for 10 years, which will be the first payment of 2009 (Jan. 28, 2009 for ARX).

06/26/09	0.100
05/27/09	0.100
04/28/09	0.120
03/27/09	0.120
02/25/09	0.120
01/28/09	0.120
12/29/08	0.150
11/26/08	0.200

4. If you go past the January 2009 date, move the mouse back up, not releasing the left mouse button. ***If you don't get the section highlighted you will have to try again.**

5. When you have the January 28, 2009 date and dividend paid highlighted, release the left mouse button.

6. To copy the highlighted data, hold the "Ctrl" button down and press the letter "C". **Ctrl C is copy.**

7. Go to the Excel worksheet and open the "20 Mo Div" worksheet as ARX's dividend is monthly.

8. Click on the cell to the right of "Copy Data >" and below "Monthly Dividends".

	Monthly Dividends
Copy Data >	

9. Hold the "Ctrl" key and press "V". **Ctrl V is to paste.**

	Monthly Dividends	
Copy Data >	12/28/2018	0.05
	11/29/2018	0.05
	10/30/2018	0.05
	9/27/2018	0.05
	8/30/2018	0.05
	7/30/2018	0.05
	6/28/2018	0.05
	5/30/2018	0.05
	4/27/2018	0.05
	3/28/2018	0.05
	2/27/2018	0.05
	1/30/2018	0.05	0.60

10. This worksheet allows for 20 monthly companies (70 companies for quarterly dividends) to be entered. Each is listed below the first, so you would arrow down to the next section for the next company paying a monthly dividend.

ARX	29-Dec-09	29-Dec-10	28-Dec-11	27-Dec-12	27-Dec-13	29-Dec-14	29-Dec-15	28-Dec-16	28-Dec-17	28-Dec-18	10 Yr Gth%
Dividend	1.28	1.20	1.20	1.20	1.20	1.20	1.20	0.65	0.60	0.60	**-53.13%**
Div Gth Yr		-6.25%	0.00%	0.00%	0.00%	0.00%	0.00%	-45.83%	-7.69%	0.00%	
Price											10yr Ave Yld
Yield %	#DIV/0!	#DIV/0!	#DIV/0!	#DIV/0!	#DIV/0!	#DIV/0!	#DIV/0!	#DIV/0!	#DIV/0!	#DIV/0!	#DIV/0!
Current Yld	#DIV/0!										

11. The data will be summarized above with the "10 YrGth%" calculated:

Note: If the company has not paid a dividend for 10 years the worksheet will not calculate the data correctly, instead you'll see this:

BIP.UN has only started paying a dividend since 2010, so you will see "#DIVO!", where the worksheet cannot calculate the formula.

BIP.UN	0-Jan-00	24-Feb-10	27-May-11	29-Aug-12	28-Aug-13	27-Aug-14	25-Nov-15	28-Nov-16	29-Nov-17	29-Nov-18	10 Yr Gth%
Dividend	0.00	0.20	0.76	0.96	1.12	1.36	1.68	2.05	2.26	2.44	#DIV/0!
Div Gth Yr		#DIV/0!	287.76%	26.32%	16.98%	20.66%	24.21%	22.04%	9.93%	8.02%	

M104		f_x	=(L104-C104)/C104

B	C	D	E	F	
BIP.UN	0-Jan-00	24-Feb-10	27-May-11	29-Aug-12	2
Dividend	0.00	0.20	0.76	0.96	
Div Gth Yr		#DIV/0!	287.76%	26.32%	

If you wanted to correct the "10YrGth%" cell you need to edit the formula, which is currently

We have to change both the "C104" to "D104", which is the 2010 column where the first dividend was paid.

| M104 | | fx =(L104-D104)/D104 | | | | | | | | | |

B	C	D	E	F	G	H	I	J	K	L	M
BIP.UN	0-Jan-00	24-Feb-10	27-May-11	29-Aug-12	28-Aug-13	27-Aug-14	25-Nov-15	28-Nov-16	29-Nov-17	29-Nov-18	10 Yr Gth%
Dividend	0.00	0.20	0.76	0.96	1.12	1.36	1.68	2.05	2.26	2.44	1144.39%
Div Gth Yr		#DIV/0!	287.76%	26.32%	16.98%	20.66%	24.21%	22.04%	9.93%	8.02%	

Note: If you feel you need to record dividend data for more than 70 quarterly ("70 QtrDiv") and 20 monthly companies ("20 Mo Div"), you can copy either of the worksheets into a new worksheet. Here's how:

1. Click at the top left of the "70" or "20" worksheets.

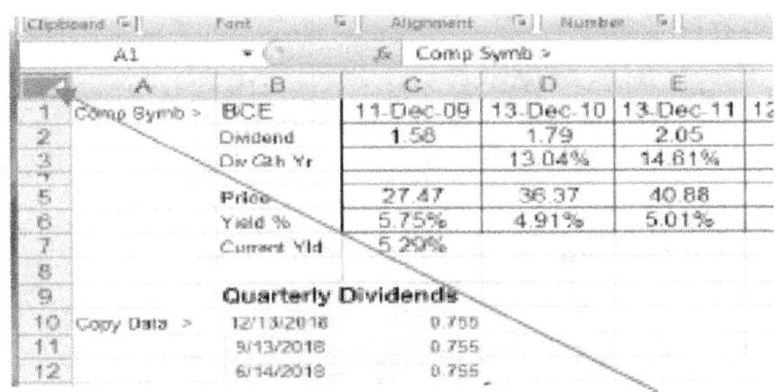

The space next to "A" and up from "1".

2. By clicking it you will highlight the entire worksheet. Now hold down "Ctrl" key and press "C" (**Ctrl C is to copy**).

3. At the bottom click the tab "Sheet 1".

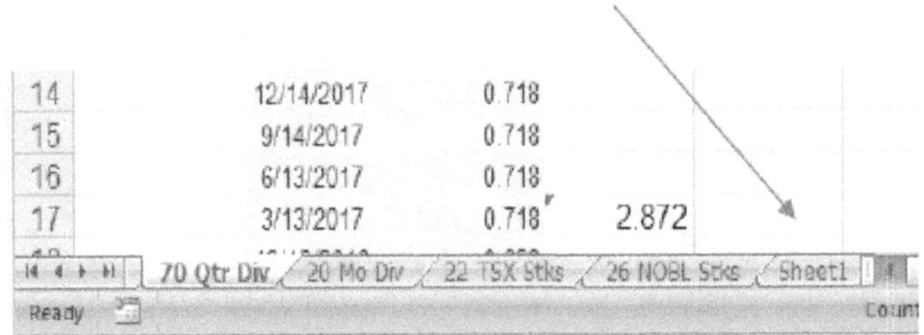

4. This will open up a new worksheet, and then hold the "Ctrl" key down and press "V" (**Ctrl V to paste**).

5. You will now have a duplicate of the "70 QtrDiv" or "20 Mo Div" worksheet you copied.

6. You can rename the worksheet by pressing your right mouse key on "Sheet 1" then press the left mouse key on "Rename". Now type what you want to name the worksheet.

7. You can repeat the process if you want to do the same for the other Monthly or Quarterly worksheet.

Note: Some may find the above process very labour intensive and too difficult. Rather than disregard using the Dividend Channel process as I described, you could instead add up the dividends for each quarter or month and enter the yearly dividend amounts in the "% GthYld" worksheet as we explained with the Morningstar process.

You would still need to obtain the yearly closing price for each stock (using the Yahoo website) to have the worksheet calculate the "10-year Average Yield" percentage.

3rd. Alternative for dividend data

Dividend Growth Investing and Retirement

https://www.dividendgrowthinvestingandretirement.com/canadian-dividend-all-star-list/

If one signs up (free) at the *Dividend Growth Investing & Retirement* website you can download their *Canadian Dividend All-Star List* (which is updated periodically). The dividend listing goes back to 2002 for those companies that have paid and raised their dividend five or more years consecutively.

This website offers a great list of Canadian companies; however, a stock is removed from the list if for any reason it does not raise their dividend for a year. This eliminated the Canadian banks during the financial crisis, until they met the 5 years of consecutive dividend increases again.

This list is very useful because it lists the companies by the longest number of years that they have raised their dividend, but still run the 4-Rule test on them. I think you'll find that

Canadian Dividend All-Star List

http://www.dividendgrowthinvestingandretirement.com/canadian-divide June 28th

Seq	Ticker	Company	Streak	Price
1	CU.TO	Canadian Utilities	47	$ 36.96
2	FTS.TO	Fortis Inc	45	$ 51.71
3	TIH.TO	Toromont Industries Ltd	29	$ 62.07
4	CWB.TO	Canadian Western Bank	27	$ 29.87
5	ACO-X.TO	Atco Ltd., Cl.I,	25	$ 44.14
6	TRI.TO	Thomson Reuters	25	$ 84.48
		Div in USD, so yield adj @ 1 USD = 1.3		
7	EMP-A.TO	Empire Company Ltd	24	$ 32.98
8	IMO.TO	Imperial Oil	24	$ 36.26
9	MRU.TO	Metro Inc	24	$ 49.14
10	CNR.TO	Canadian National Railway	23	$ 121.20
11	ENB.TO	Enbridge Inc	23	$ 47.30

even with consecutive dividend increases, some won't make your "List of Stocks to Consider".

When you open the excel file, **scroll all the way right** until you see the years with the annual dividends listed, as shown

Company	2018	2017	2016	2015	2014	2013
Canadian Utilities	$1.5732	$1.4300	$1.3000	$1.1800	$1.0700	$0.9700
Fortis Inc	$1.7250	$1.6250	$1.5250	$1.3950	$1.2800	$1.2400
Toromont Industries Ltd	$0.9200	$0.7600	$0.7200	$0.6800	$0.6000	$0.5200
Canadian Western Bank	$1.0200	$0.9400	$0.9200	$0.8800	$0.8000	$0.7200
Atco Ltd., Cl.I.	$1.5064	$1.3100	$1.1400	$0.9900	$0.8600	$0.7500

below.

Further to the right you'll see the highest yield percentages, which could be used to calculate the 10-year average yields.

We'll use the "Div Gth" tab in our worksheet to type in the

idend All-Star List	Highest Yield 2018	Highest Yield 2017	Highest Yield 2016	Highest Yield 2015	Highest Yield 2014	Highest Yield 2013
dgrowthinvestingandretirement.com/canad Company						
Canadian Utilities	5.48%	4.15%	4.30%	4.00%	3.03%	2.90%
Fortis Inc	4.48%	4.17%	4.29%	4.08%	4.30%	4.20%
Toromont Industries Ltd	2.03%	1.88%	2.64%	2.55%	2.45%	2.46%
Canadian Western Bank	4.19%	4.09%	4.78%	4.18%	2.77%	2.66%
Atco Ltd., Cl.I.	4.36%	3.05%	3.44%	2.98%	1.98%	1.89%

10-year dividends and the yields, which will calculate the 10-year"Gth/Yld Ave" percentage and the 10-year"Ave Yield". I'll enter FTS (Fortis) figures for this example:

FTS	2009	2010	2011	2012	2013	2014	2015	2016	2017	2018	Gth/Yld Ave
Dividend	1.04	1.12	1.16	1.20	1.24	1.28	1.40	1.53	1.63	1.73	65.87%
Ave Yld	4.81%	4.35%	3.98%	3.77%	4.20%	4.30%	4.08%	4.29%	4.17%	4.48%	4.24%

Div Gth | %Gth Yld | TSX60 | NOBL | 70 Qtr Div | 20 Mo Div | Stks Consider | NOBL Stks | Sheet1

You can follow the same process to enter any of the other stocks from the Dividend All-Star list.

I've provided three different sources to find and enter the dividend data into the Excel worksheets, which you will then evaluate and decide which stocks should make your "List of Stocks to Consider". There may be other web sources which will provide the same data, so don't feel you need to restrict yourself to just the sources I mentioned, but check the data or at least compare with the other sources, especially when the source is US, which may not have completely accurate figures for Canadian stocks.

When you have finished your analysis of all the TSX60 stocks, you may wish to compare your results to mine.

I eliminated 43 of the TSX 60 at first, but after applying the exception rules, I added 5 back in, resulting in a final tally of 22 quality stocks out of 60 which made my "List of Stocks to Consider" worksheet.

There is no right or wrong answer on how many stocks you eliminate or keep. I think less is better if you are just starting your TFSA income investment journey. I want to keep things simple by sticking with the best dividend growth stocks you can find.

You do not have to buy or even consider buying all the stocks on your "List of Stocks to Consider" for your TFSA, you are just compiling a list of stocks to choose from, when they are reasonably priced (which is discussed later). When it comes to purchasing stocks, it will be much easier to choose from 15 or 20 than 60.

As I mentioned before there will always be exceptions on whether to add a stock or not. Consider each on their unique merits. I'd rather you feel you've selected the best, not the most. I hope you, like me, will be attracted to the "Steady

Eddies"; these are the stocks with a long history of sharing their earnings, these stocks increase their payout to shareholders each year. Again, you do not have to buy or consider buying all the stocks on your list. You are just determining potential companies to purchase so you don't have to look for new stocks or consider stocks which you have not evaluated.

I'll talk more about dividend growth later, but if you find a company that increases their dividend each year, even if it's only by as little as 5%, remember that it is this percentage increase that will build your TFSA future wealth. The growth may begin slowly, but the longer you hold the stocks and the more funds you add over time, the faster your income will grow. **We are not looking for or expecting short-term quick growth, but long-term sustained growth.**

Also, we are not trying to compile the largest list of good stocks, instead we're making a short list of the best stocks to choose from. Through sorting and screening you will try to identify a list of the best-of-the-best!

Personal Note: The four-rule test is much more important than it may seem at first glance. It almost seems too simple to believe that it actually works, but I can confirm that it really does. Use it every chance you get to analyze any stock or stocks within a fund. I think you'll come to the same conclusion I have, that the four-rule test is an easy and quick way to determine if a company is a quality income (dividend) growth stock. That's our main focus, finding stocks that will generate the income you seek and provide the compounding growth we need for your *TFSA "Compounder"*.

A few other things to consider

By performing the four-rule test on the TSX 60 stocks, you might be satisfied with the list generated as is, but there are a few more things you might wish to examine before making your final selections. The following section will concentrate on this next level of analysis:

Checking a company's long-term dividend history chart

To check the "Long-Term Dividend Charts" of companies, go to The Dividend Channel online: https://www.canadastockchannel.com/

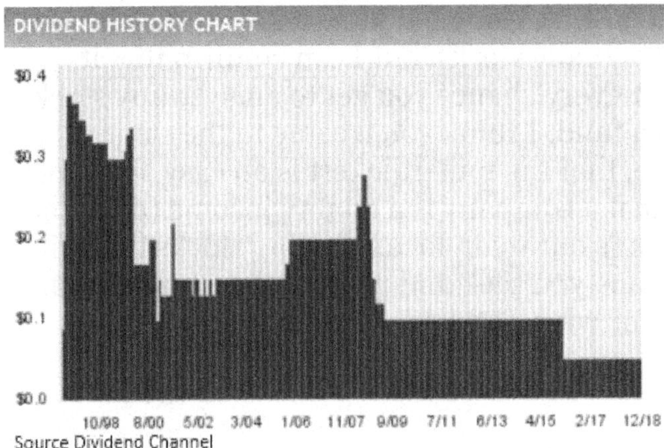

For Canadian stocks and funds add .CA after the symbol. We are checking stocks on the TSX 60, and I will use ARX Resources (ARX) as an example. You may not wish to check all the stocks you have eliminated, but you should check a few just to confirm your initial findings.

Enter the company symbol "ARX.CA", and review the chart illustrating its dividend history (I have provided a screenshot of the chart above).

If you remember, I easily eliminated ARX using the four-rule test, for cutting their dividend, and after looking at its 20-year dividend chart, it confirms my initial decision. This demonstrates the importance of dividend growth in choosing quality stocks. It also helps to see a company's growth pattern in a visual form, I find these charts very useful as an "at a glance" reference.

Now let's look at BCE.CA's dividend growth history.

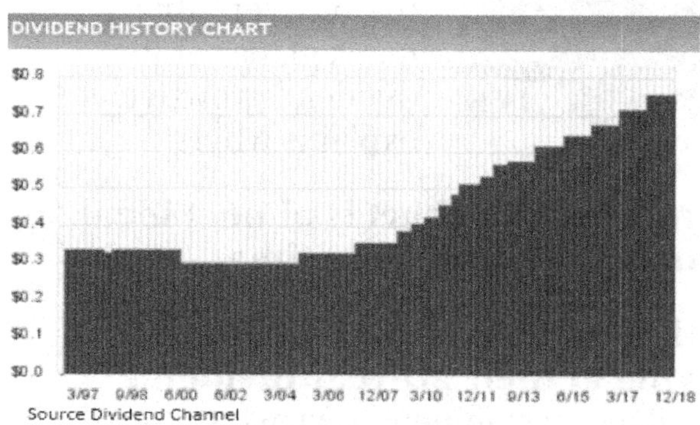

BCE is an example of a four-rule "yes" stock on my list. BCE shows a good dividend growth chart, despite a flat period between 1997 and 2005, there is a steady dividend increase after that.

I also want to provide two other examples with AEM and BNS. AEM was first on the TSX 60 list. It cut the dividend but had a dividend growth rate of 144%. But if you look at its

Name	Symbol	Div Cuts Yes/No	Pd Div 10Yrs Yes/No	Raised Div 10yrs Yes/No	Start Div	Ending Div	Div Gth 75% over 10yrs	Current Yield	Consider Pur Yes/No and Cor
Barrick Gold Corp	ABX	Yes	Yes	No	0.40	0.12	-70.00%	0.89%	No, Div Cut
Agnico Eagle Mines Limited	AEM	Yes	Yes	No	0.18	0.44	144.44%	0.98%	No, Div Cut
Bank of Nova Scotia	BNS	No	Yes	No 9 of 10	1.96	3.28	67.35%	4.79%	Yes, Exception

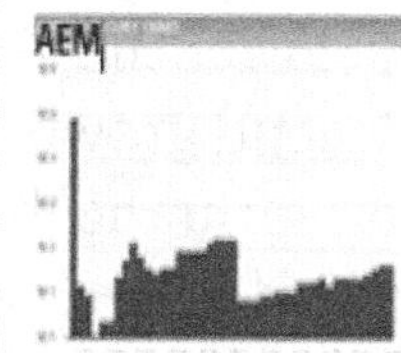

dividend chart below, you will see how it confirms that it is actually not a quality dividend growth stock:

The AEM dividend growth was a result of an extremely low dividend in 2008. However, the chart shows that there has been no real dividend growth since 2007.

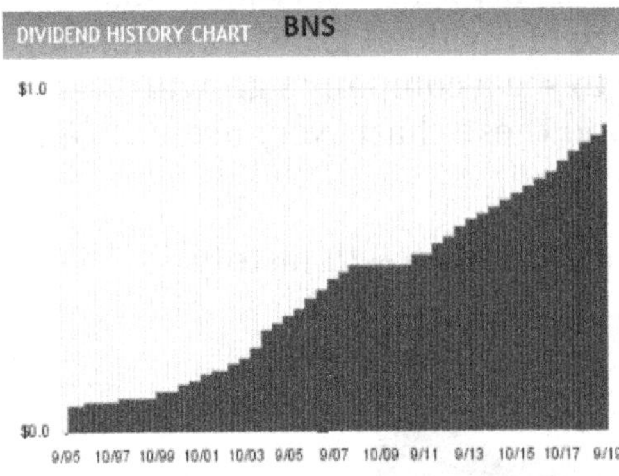

Now look at BNS's chart: Even with only a 67.35% 10-year dividend growth rate, BNS is one I added back on to my "List of Stocks to Consider". Just a quick glance at its dividend growth chart explains why!

The BNS long-term dividend chart is almost ideal, a steady and continuous increase over time.

I recommend applying the four-rule test to the stocks before looking at their 20-year dividend chart. As much as I like to recommend reviewing charts, sometimes they can be deceiving, depending upon how they are presented and the number spread used on the chart. The four-rule test and 10-year analysis provides a clearer picture of a company's current status. Use the Dividend Channel charts to view a longer time period, especially for those stocks you might have listed as "exceptions", or when you might want to take another look at a stock that didn't initially make your list.

Low Yield, High Dividend growth

The lower the yield, the less current income, but if the dividend growth is at a higher rate, then over the long-term the dividend growth will likely drive the price of the stock higher.

With this step I want to demonstrate how a low-dividend yield, with a high-dividend growth record may be acceptable for long-term investors. Using Morningstar.ca, let's look at Canadian National Railway's (CNR) current yield as an example.

CNR	2009	2010	2011	2012	2013	2014	2015	2016	2017	2018	Gth/Yld Ave
Dividend	0.51	0.54	0.65	0.75	0.86	1.00	1.25	1.50	1.65	1.82	**256.86%**
% chg		5.88%	20.37%	15.38%	14.67%	16.28%	25.00%	20.00%	10.00%	10.30%	**15.32%**
Price	28.98	33.13	40.12	45.18	60.56	80	77.16	90.36	103.77	101.11	
Yield	1.76%	1.63%	1.62%	1.66%	1.42%	1.25%	1.62%	1.66%	1.59%	1.80%	**1.60%**

If you had entered the yearly dividends and prices for CNR in the "%GthYld" worksheet during your initial evaluation, here's what it would look like. Also look at the "% Chg" row and see the percentage growth of the dividend each year. The 15.32% at the end is the average percentage growth.

As of this writing, the current yield is 1.74%, which is a bit higher than the past 10 years and its 10-year average of 1.60%. This indicates that the price has gone down which makes it slightly less expensive. I consider CNR a good stock to buy when the current yield is above the 10-year average.

Why a good stock's yield is 3% above its average yield

For the stocks which make your "List of Stocks to Consider", the higher current yield above the 10-year average means the stock is cheaper and offers higher income than normal.

But what if the current dividend yield is 3-4% above their 10-year average dividend yield? This is not an extremely high yield difference, but it should make one proceed with caution.

Enbridge (ENB) is a good example of this situation. Morningstar shows, as of this writing, that ENB's current yield is 6.40% and its 10-year average dividend yield is 3.24%

With its current yield of 6.40%, this is 2.79% higher than the average 10-year yield by 3.61%. Could this be considered a problem?

ENB	2009	2010	2011	2012	2013	2014	2015	2016	2017	2018	Gth/Yld Ave
Dividend	0.74	1.08	0.98	1.13	1.26	1.40	1.86	2.12	2.41	2.68	**262.16%**
% chg		43.24%	-7.55%	15.31%	11.50%	11.11%	32.86%	13.98%	13.68%	11.20%	**16.15%**
Price	24.32	28.64	38.09	43.02	46.41	59.74	46.00	56.5	49.16	42.41	
Yield	3.04%	3.77%	2.57%	2.63%	2.71%	2.34%	4.04%	3.75%	4.90%	6.32%	3.61%

If you followed the news during this period, you'd know that there was concern about ENB's debt level. Management acknowledged the high debt and promised to sell assets and reduce expenses, which they have. But the market has been weak for all pipelines so the price of ENB has remained low, thus providing a high current yield. In this case, one should look further into the company's debt and the action they've taken, if any, to correct the debt problem. Regardless, one might feel ENB is still a solid stock, its dividend is safe and that this is an opportunity to buy its shares at a discounted price and increase one's income. If you find yourself comfortable with the decisions of management to deal with these financial challenges, then you could proceed to purchase. Remember, the decision is yours.

Consider a company's Payout Ratio

Payout ratio is the portion of the company's annual earnings being paid out as dividends. To find a business's dividend-payout ratio for a given time period, use either the formula of dividends paid divided by net income, or calculate yearly dividends per share divided by earnings per share. These two formulas are equivalent to each other.

For most companies 60% to 75% is a reasonable maximum payout ratio, but utility companies usually go higher, around 80%. So, there is no fixed or average payout ratio which you can apply to all stocks.

Possibly one of the best guides would be to compare the current payout ratio to other stocks in the same sector. For example, if you were considering buying BCE you could determine the payout ratio for Telus and Rogers and see how they compare to BCE's payout ratio.

You could also look at the 10-year payout ratios for BCE,

BCE Inc BCE | ★★★

Financials

Export 📄 Ascending

	2009-12	2010-12	2011-12	2012-12	2013-12	2014-12	2015-12	2016-12	2017-12	2018-12
Revenue CAD Mil	17,735	18,069	19,497	18,975	20,400	21,042	21,514	21,719	22,719	23,468
Gross Margin %	74.5	72.6	39.1	48.5	48.8	48.5	48.4	49.3	49.1	49.5
Operating Income CAD Mil	3,718	3,896	3,959	4,495	4,709	4,851	5,131	5,280	5,329	5,441
Operating Margin %	21.0	21.6	20.3	22.5	23.1	23.1	23.8	24.3	23.5	23.3
Net Income CAD Mil	1,738	2,277	2,348	2,763	2,106	2,500	2,678	3,031	2,914	2,929
Earnings Per Share CAD	2.11	2.74	2.88	3.17	2.54	1.97	2.98	3.33	3.20	3.10
Dividends CAD	1.58	1.78	2.04	2.22	2.33	2.47	2.62	2.73	2.87	3.02
Payout Ratio % *	74.5	63.8	71.4	65.5	77.4	81.8	85.6	85.3	87.8	97.8
Shares Mil	772	769	771	775	776	795	848	870	894	898
Book Value Per Share * CAD	18.51	19.19	13.57	13.52	14.95	12.66	14.07	14.28	17.00	18.72
Operating Cash Flow CAD Mil	4,875	4,724	4,869	5,552	6,476	6,241	6,274	6,643	7,358	7,354
Cap Spending CAD Mil	-2,854	-2,959	-3,256	-3,515	-3,571	-4,283	-4,161	-3,772	-4,034	-4,027
Free Cash Flow CAD Mil	2,021	1,765	1,613	2,037	2,905	1,958	2,113	2,871	3,324	3,357
Free Cash Flow Per Share * CAD	2.61	2.33	2.14	2.63	2.77	1.83	2.37	3.34	3.71	3.45

which are listed just below the dividends at Morningstar:

Another statistic we can utilize in our analysis is the "Free Cash Flow" and "Free Cash Flow per Share", which can be seen lower down on the "Key Stats" screen. Free cash flow is the cash left over after a company pays for its operating expenses and capital expenditures, which means they will have cash to pay the dividend even if earnings were low. When I calculate what the percentage is of the Free Cash Flow to BCEs dividend, it seems low, but not out of line with other years:

BCE	2009	2010	2011	2012	2013	2014	2015	2016	2017	2018
Dividend	1.58	1.78	2.04	2.22	2.33	2.47	2.6	2.73	2.87	3.02
Free C/F	2.61	2.33	2.14	2.63	2.77	2.83	2.37	3.34	3.71	3.45
%	65.19%	30.90%	4.90%	18.47%	18.88%	14.57%	-8.85%	22.34%	29.27%	14.24%

Avoid high yield stocks

Stocks with a high dividend yield, in my opinion anything above 7%, may have difficulty maintaining the dividend or may even cut it, or not raise the dividend over time.

Corus Entertainment (CJR.B) will make a good example of this.

CJR.B	2009	2010	2011	2012	2013	2014	2015	2016	2017	2018	Gth/Yld Ave
Dividend	0.6	0.6	0.76	0.93	1	1.07	1.12	1.14	1.14	1.04	**73.33%**
% chg		0.00%	26.67%	22.37%	7.53%	7.00%	4.67%	1.79%	0.00%	-8.77%	
Price	18.6	22.45	20.83	25.42	24.94	24.73	21.57	9.73	12.92	5.57	
Yield	3.23%	2.67%	3.65%	3.66%	4.01%	4.33%	5.19%	11.72%	8.82%	18.67%	6.59%

Upon entering the CJR's dividend yields from Morningstar in your Excel spreadsheet, you will see that the last three years, Corus' yield was 11.72%, 8.82% and 18.67%. These are well above 7% and likely unsustainable. From 2009 to 2015 the average yield was 3.82%, so when it jumped to a double digit yield, it was just a matter of time before the dividend would be cut, which Corus did in September 2018 by 75%.

Avoid cyclical stocks

Finally, I mentioned avoiding cyclical stocks earlier, now I'd like to explain further. Cyclical stocks are those affected by the ups and downs in the overall economy, such as airline, auto, technology, most energy, retail, consumer and mining stocks. When applying the four-rule test to cyclical stocks on the TSX 60, you will most likely have found they were quickly eliminated, mainly because they normally cut their dividend when they are on a down cycle.

Even if you are willing to take chances on stocks that do not fit my criteria, I recommend you avoid stocks that fall into the definition of cyclical.

Once you've put any of these considerations to practical use and seen how they affect any of the stocks on your "List of Stocks to Consider", you may wish to add, remove or just make a note for future reference.

Follow the same four-step evaluation process for any other stock which may not be listed on the TSX60.

Evaluation tools not considered

It might be a good time to note that we have not looked at many of the other common stock evaluation methods, such as:

- Price to Earnings (P/E), Price to Sales and Price to Cash flow, Return on Equity.
- Estimating the intrinsic value of a stock, the discounted value of the cash that can be taken out of a business during its remaining life.
- Margin metrics, Gross Margin, Operating and Net.
- The Discounted Cash flow, future cash flows are estimated and discounted by using cost of capital to give their present values.

Most of these are used to determine if a stock is expensive, value priced, and/or to project its future earnings potential. Are they useful? Maybe, but they are more likely to be useful when one is seeking price growth from investments rather than income. This is also not a definitive list, there are as many ways to research and evaluate stocks as there are stock strategies to choose from.

Dividends are real and relevant markers, meaning the company either has the cash to pay the dividend or it does not. Reported earnings, on the other hand, may or may not be actual. I feel comfortable with the handful of steps I have provided and my experience with this method over the years. The point I am trying to make is that my strategy is about simplification, but again I must stress that your comfort level is the priority, feel free to research as many forms of analysis as you wish.

I have narrowed a fairly large selection of companies to a few key dividend growth stocks using yield and dividend growth as our key evaluation measurement. I then applied even more tests for further consideration. It isn't a perfect test, but I do believe that by following the process I've outlined and by adding some common sense for good measure, you should feel comfortable with your results.

Your "**List of Stocks to Consider**" for your TFSA should now be complete, (unless you wish to apply the four-rules to other stocks outside of the TSX 60). The next steps are:

- Group the stocks into sectors (banks, consumer, pipeline, telecom, utility, etc.).
- Record the information on the "Stks Consider" worksheet and group them by sector.
- When you are ready to buy, consider the stock(s), in the same sector, that is currently less expensive, or at least offering a better yield than the others.
- You may wish to enter "Suggested Buy Prices" in the "Stks Consider" worksheet to determine possible yields at various prices.
- Remember, you do not have to own every stock on your list. You may start with a utility or telecom. Next you may buy a bank or pipeline and so on.
- Be aware that individual stocks and sectors will vary in price at different times.
- We are looking to purchase at a reasonable price or yield, which we will discuss later in the book.
- Once you've got 3 to 5 stocks in three or four sectors in your TFSA you might wish to stick with those for a while, adding to them when the price or yield is attractive.
- If the market has a correction you may be enticed to buy a particular stock which always seemed expensive but is now more reasonable.

- I'd like to reiterate a point I will make often. I'd rather have a lot invested in a few good stocks, rather than the same amount (or more) in a large group of mediocre stocks. Less is more.

"Stocks to Consider" worksheet

I suggested above you record the stocks which passed your Four-Rule test onto the "Stks Consider" worksheet, grouping them by sector. I know this is duplicating some of the entries, but this worksheet will provide information to assist you in deciding when to purchase particular stocks you are considering.

The chart below is just a sample and you would enter the

	List of Stocks to Consider			Start Div	Ending Div	10 Yr Div Gth%	10 Yr Ave Yield	Current Div	Current Price	Current Yield	Suggested Buy Price	Yield %	Suggested Buy Price	Yield %	Suggested Buy Price	Yield %
1	Bank of Nova Scotia	BNS	Bank	1.96	3.28	67.35%	3.97%	3.48	$71.91	4.84%	$67.00	5.19%	$66.50	5.23%	$66.00	5.27%
2	Royal Bank	RY	Bank	2.00	3.77	88.50%	3.76%	3.77	$107.26	3.51%	$106.50	3.54%	$106.00	3.56%	$105.00	3.59%
2	BCE	BCE	Commun	1.58	3.02	91.14%	4.94%	3.17	$63.37	5.00%	$63.90	4.96%	$63.45	5.00%	$63.00	5.03%
3	Telus	T	Commun			#DIV/0!						#DIV/0!		#DIV/0!		#DIV/0!

updated data when you are ready to consider buying.

You would update the following:

- Current annual dividend,
- Current Price, and
- Add three "Suggested Buy Prices".

When you enter the suggested buy prices it will calculate the expected "Yield" in the next column. By entering different prices and comparing the yields to the 10-year average yield for the stock, you will have an idea if the current yield is reasonable if purchased at one of those prices (the higher the current yield the better).

In one of my examples using BNS, the current price is $71.91, so I entered $71.00, $70.50 and $71.50 (a higher price). Even the highest price is above the 10-year average yield, which is 3.97%. This indicates the current price is a reasonable price to buy at.

When you look at Royal Bank, the current yield is below the 10-year average and the price would have to drop considerably to become above the 10-year average, or the dividend would have to be increased.

But yield is only part of your decision when deciding to buy. Dividend growth is the other factor to consider, and possibly more important than the current yield.

We listed the stocks by sector so you can compare them and possibly identify the one(s) offering the highest (reasonable) yield and a good growth rate. Compare the 10-year average growth as well as the past three years' year-to-year dividend growth percentage of each stock in each sector.

BNS	2009	2010	2011	2012	2013	2014	2015	2016	2017	2018	Gth/Yld Ave
Dividend	1.96	1.96	2.05	2.19	2.39	2.56	2.72	2.88	3.05	3.28	67.35%
% Chg		0.00%	4.59%	6.83%	9.13%	7.11%	6.25%	5.88%	5.90%	7.54%	
Price	44.83	56.46	51.53	58.65	63.32	66.81	57.39	77.76	81.72	74.8	
Yield	4.37%	3.47%	3.98%	3.73%	3.77%	3.83%	4.74%	3.70%	3.73%	4.39%	3.97%

RY	2009	2010	2011	2012	2013	2014	2015	2016	2017	2018	Gth/Yld Ave
Dividend	2.00	2.00	2.08	2.28	2.53	2.84	3.08	3.24	3.48	3.77	88.50%
% Chg		0.00%	4.00%	9.62%	10.96%	12.25%	8.45%	5.19%	7.41%	8.33%	
Price	56.81	54.95	47.26	58.9	70.44	83.16	75.27	87.08	100.85	97.42	
Yield	3.52%	3.64%	4.40%	3.87%	3.59%	3.42%	4.09%	3.72%	3.45%	3.87%	3.76%

When looking at BNS and Royal Bank, BNS is offering a higher current yield, but Royal Bank has a higher 10-year dividend growth. As for the past three years' dividend growth percentage, Royal Bank has been a slightly higher. So, they are fairly close and you would have to decide which you like best.

For BCE the current yield of 5%, which is just above its 10-year average yield of 4.94%, one might like to see the price fall a bit. If BCE's price were to rise to $64.00 it would almost match the 10-year average yield.

If you had other communication stocks on your list you would compare the results with them and make your "buy" decision as to which would be the best, comparing current yield to the 10-year average yield, etc.

Comparing the current yield or an estimated yield if the price drops to the 10-year average yield and the year-to-year percentage is a quick method of determining if the current price is at a reasonable price to buy. We'll discuss other methods later in the book.

During the stock evaluation process you may wish to develop your own criteria, which may vary from mine. I am suggesting guidelines, not strict rules, and the final decision on which stocks qualify or not is yours.

With your list complete, ignore all other Canadian stocks that did not make your list! This is important because I want you to remain focused. You've done the work, made your selection, now concentrate on generating income from those stocks.

Personal Note: In my opinion one does not need to own a lot of stocks to generate a large and growing income. I hold four stocks in my TFSA and my wife has five. We have invested the maximum amounts each January since 2009 and will not likely add many other stocks to our TFSAs. Later in Chapter 4 we'll compare our actual 10-year TFSA results with the projected results of following the *TFSA "Compounder"* investment strategy.

In our entire portfolio we hold only twelve company stocks, though we do have several of the same company stocks in different accounts. For example, we hold the same bank stock in one RRIF, a TFSA, Joint and a DRIP account.

The decision on how many stocks to own is a personal choice, my only recommendation is to stick with quality dividend growth stocks which meet your evaluation criteria.

Let's evaluate the XIU ETF

I mentioned earlier in my book that I do not recommend investing in ETFs (Exchange Traded Funds) for income, and it is only fair that I provide you with some specifics and hope you will come to the same conclusion.

XIU is the ETF which holds the same 60 stocks as the TSX 60. I used the TSX 60 as our source of companies to find qualifying stocks and applied the four-rule test to find our recommended dividend growth stocks. In my own analysis, I was able to eliminate 38 companies or 63.33% (23 Cut their dividend, 7 paid no dividend and 8 had low dividend growth) of the original 60, and I expect you will come close to the same number with your calculations.

By analyzing the entire XIU ETF, we can see what it would be like to invest in all 60 stocks, rather than only the best income providers of the group.

To start, we will go to The Dividend Channel website to check the XIU's 18-year distributions chart: Enter "XIU.CA" where it says "Enter Symbol".

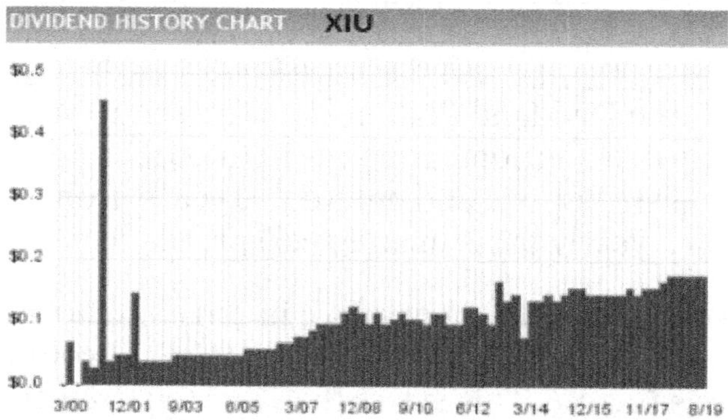

Scroll down to see the 18-year Distribution chart:

As you can see there does not appear to have been much distribution (income) growth over the past 18 years for this particular ETF.

Now compare XIU with a single stock, I will use BCE's 18-

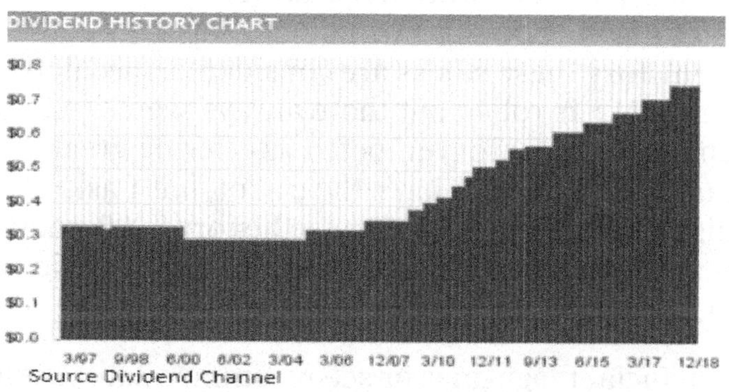

year dividend chart for this example:

When you compare the XIU distribution chart to BCE, XIU comes out the loser. Feel free to check some of the other companies' dividend charts from your "List of Stocks to Consider" and compare them to XIU.

XIU	25-Sep-09	27-Sep-10	25-Mar-11	21-Sep-12	18-Sep-13	17-Sep-14	16-Sep-15	23-Nov-16	22-Nov-17	27-Nov-18	10 Yr Gth%
Dividend	0.43	0.45	0.44	0.48	0.53	0.57	0.61	0.45	0.62	0.69	61.12%
Div Gth Yr		4.45%	-0.67%	8.80%	9.75%	7.56%	7.73%	-25.94%	37.44%	10.26%	

Further down on the Dividend Channel you can see 18 years of XIU's quarterly distributions, from 2000 to 2018. I added up the quarterly distributions and entered 10 years, from 2009 to 2018, on a yearly basis in an Excel spreadsheet.

Notice that the distributions are negative in 2011 and 2016 (the distribution dropped), and under the "10 YrGth" column you see it listed as 61.12%. This is less than our required 75% 10-year dividend growth requirement from our four-rule test.

With low dividend growth and distribution cuts, that's a double whammy, or one might apply author Stephen King's quote: *"Fool me once, shame on you. Fool me twice, shame on me"*.

I don't think many would recommend investing in a new stock (IPO) for income, because without an earnings and performance history these stocks are considered speculative. Yet when a new ETF is rolled out there always seems to be a lot of excitement as they are trumpeted as offering great diversification and low fees. That's the carrot, but I ask where the distribution and performance history is? Perhaps they are not as speculative as an IPO but I feel they are just as uncertain, especially for an Income investor.

If you read financial magazines or see recommendations for various ETFs, take the time to look at their distribution history, calculate the distribution growth percentage and look carefully for distribution cuts. Also remember that distributions are not all dividends and, therefore, the returns may be misleading. Better yet, just ignore all the hype with regards to ETFs and concentrate on the income you can receive from the smaller group of stocks you have identified through your own analysis.

If I haven't quite been able to convince you why, as an Income investor, you should avoid ETFs in your TFSA, here is one more example I hope will do the trick. Vanguard Canada is one of the country's largest ETF providers. They have added five new ETFs, created by combining several of their existing ETFs:

1. The Conservative Income ETF (VCIP) holds 80% bonds and 20% stocks.
2. The Conservative ETF (VCNS) holds 60% bonds and 40% stocks.
3. The Balanced ETF (VBAL) holds 60% stocks and 40% bonds.
4. The Aggressive ETF (VGRO) holds 80% stocks and 20% bonds.
5. The All-Equity ETF (VEQT) is 100% stocks.

On the outside, these "All-in-One" ETFs would seem to offer something for everyone. Proclaimed as total simplicity with low fees, one no longer needs to worry about diversification, asset allocation and rebalancing. They claim to take care of it all, but I am simply not convinced of the benefits of these ETFs.

Perhaps an analogy will better help illustrate my point:

A man walks into a bar and asks for a glass of the best whiskey in the house, with water. The bartender carefully measures one ounce of his best spirit, then... abruptly pours it into a gallon of water and stirs! He nonchalantly pours out a glass, passes it to the man, and without a hint of irony says, "The first glass is on the house".

All five of the Vanguard funds have more than a whopping twelve thousand holdings each! Yes, each of these funds hold 12,637 stocks and/or bonds, and trying to identify the best of their holdings might be akin to being able to taste the whiskey in that glass.

Chapter 3

Just because everyone else believes it...

When talking about a beginners' guide to investing or Investing 101, "Diversification", "Asset Allocation" and "Rebalancing" are often considered fundamental principles of sound investing. You will also hear terms like Time Horizon, Risk Tolerance, Risk vs Reward, Investment Choices and Goals, and finally Protecting Your Capital. That's the end goal for the vast majority of investors, Capital Protection. But as an Income investor, our objective is income and income growth, so we have to ask if these basic rules automatically apply to our goals?

In this section I provide definitions to these common investing terms and explanations why they don't necessarily work within my Income investment strategy parameters.

Diversification

Common definition: "Diversification is a technique that reduces risk by allocating investments among various financial instruments, industries, and other categories. It aims to maximize return by investing in different areas that would each react differently to the same event."

Rather than argue the point, I'll quote Warren Buffett:

> *"Diversification is protection against ignorance. It makes little sense if you know what you are doing."*

In other words, if you don't have the knowledge, time or know-how to identify quality investments, then covering all your bases might be a good way to go. However, you now have the four-rule test to identify quality companies not just in Canada (to buy in your TFSA), but in the US and any other markets (for other investment accounts).

As an Income investor, and especially for your TFSA, you do not need to own stocks in all sectors or markets. We want to concentrate on owning a few of the large, stable and profitable companies with a long record of returning some of their profits to its shareholders. I believe this relieves you of having to rely on diversification to mitigate market fluctuations. Diversify by selecting among the best stocks in a few sectors. There is no need to dilute your holdings, lower your potential income or settle for below-average income returns. I'll repeat here my personal mantra: I prefer quality over quantity.

What most investors forget is that during severe market corrections, recessions and crashes, ALL investments drop in value. The financial crisis of 2008 saw the market value of most portfolios drop by 35% or more. Being diversified did not provide any protection or lessen the impact attributed to the drop in market value. This also included dividend growth portfolios. However, the difference was that dividend growth income investors did not see their income drop, though to be fair, it may have grown at a slower rate. Fixed income was no protection, as interest rates dropped as well.

For those thinking of diversifying into foreign stocks, or Emerging or International ETFs, outside of your TFSA investment, I suggest you consider the many US companies with exposure to foreign markets, like McDonald's, Procter & Gamble and Coca-Cola. Like international stocks, they generate the bulk of their income outside the US. Buying shares of US multinationals can be an effective way for investors to get exposure to the global economy with quality DG companies. Most will be listed in the NOBL ETF, but still each stock should be carefully assessed before purchasing. Only hold US stocks in an RRSP, not a TFSA, to avoid the withholding tax.

Asset Allocation

Common Definition: "Asset allocation is an investment strategy that aims to balance risk and reward by apportioning a portfolio's assets according to an individual's goals, risk tolerance and investment horizon. The three main asset classes - equities, fixed-income, and cash and equivalents - have different levels of risk and return, so each will behave differently over time."

As an Income investor, bonds, preferred stocks and other fixed assets would not make up any part of your TFSA investment portfolio. Our objective is for a growing income, not a fixed one. The risk of prices dropping is not an Income investor's concern as we'll discuss in a later section.

Fixed assets may have a place as part of one's savings or funds, often set aside for emergency or other needs, but they are not effective in growing one's income, which is our priority.

Much of this book is devoted to showing you how to screen and evaluate stocks in order to identify the best possible dividend growth stocks to choose from. Your goal should be to enhance compounding by receiving as much income as you can from your investments so that the income can be added to your initial purchases and generate more income. Fixed income will not meet our objective of a growing and compounding income.

I recommend you maintain a 100% equity income investment, with only quality dividend growth stocks for your *TFSA "Compounder"* portfolio, chosen after careful evaluation.

Rebalancing

Common Definition: "The primary goal of a rebalancing strategy is to minimize risk relative to a target asset allocation, rather than to maximize returns. A portfolio's asset allocation is the major determinant of a portfolio's risk-and-return characteristics. Yet, over time, asset classes produce different returns, so the portfolio's asset allocation changes. Therefore, to recapture the portfolio's original risk-and-return characteristics, the portfolio should be rebalanced."

Bonds and fixed income assets, again, play no part in your *TFSA "Compounder"* investment. I do recommend holding cash reserves and keeping savings separate from your investments. Once you've taken the time to research and build your *TFSA "Compounder"* income investment portfolio, the only time you should consider rebalancing is if you re-evaluate a company's performance and find it fails to meet your expectations.

It is not price movement of the various asset classes or how other assets perform over time that Income investors should be concerned with. Income investors only have one interest in the market, and that is to take advantage of price movement to increase their income. Income investors assess and attempt to reduce risk, in advance, by screening out stocks which do not meet their income-growth criteria. I feel very confident with my four-rule test, even providing for exceptions to those rules in order to find the best possible dividend growth stocks we can.

That market volatility is a good thing for the Income investor is probably the hardest concept for most investors to accept. If you bought 100 shares of a stock at $75.00 or invested $7,500 and it suddenly dropped to $50.00 per share you will see a paper loss of $2,500. With that type of a drop in price it's hard not to panic or feel as if someone just stole $2,500 from your pocket. However, if you bought the stock because it met your criteria as a good dividend growth stock and it continues to pay and grow its dividend, then hold tight. Income investors are not concerned about the value of their holdings, instead during price drops they recognize the great opportunity to buy more shares at depressed prices and receive even more income from the reinvested dividends.

If your current roster of TFSA companies continues to provide the income growth you expect and their future looks bright, there is no reason to divest yourself of any of your current shares. We want to maximize our income and avoid giving up our best holdings. If you want to increase your holdings of a particular stock or sector, buy those on your next purchase.

I also don't feel it's important to maintain an even percentage between all stocks or sectors. I don't recommend you have all your holdings in a very small number of stocks or a single sector, but I do subscribe to the motto everything in moderation. Again, it's the income that is important and if you've built up a sizable holding of one company because you were able to buy it at a value-price, all the better. Never sell a good stock that keeps paying and growing your income.

Don't be swayed by the plethora of investment advice touting diversification, asset allocation and rebalancing. Often you'll find that wherever you look, whoever you listen to and almost whatever you read, diversification, asset allocation and re-balancing will be their suggestion as the best way to protect your investments, to provide adequate returns and to ensure you will not suffer significant losses when there is a market correction.

If price gains or beating the market was our main concern, they may be correct, **but as an Income investor, Diversification, Asset Allocation and Rebalancing will only dilute and lower your potential income.** Too many stocks spoil the stew in my opinion!

Let others diversify across the board, buy and sell to their heart's desire, all in the hopes of keeping their portfolios evenly distributed. I don't object if they do, but just because everyone else believes it necessary doesn't mean I have to. I have learned through experience what is best for my income investment portfolio and what suits my income goals and I hope you experience the same results and come to the same conclusion.

What should the dividend yield be when buying?

I mentioned earlier checking a stock's current yield through the website Morningstar and comparing it to the stock's 10-year average yield to determine if the stock is reasonably priced or expensive. But how do you interpret this information and decide what yield makes a stock worth purchasing?

I feel that any stock which has a high yield, above 7% and higher, is too high. These stocks will either be speculative (offering a high yield to entice investors), or stocks which may be experiencing financial difficulty (causing the price of the stock to drop and its yield to rise). Stocks and other investments offering a high current yield will not likely provide any income growth, in other words, you are back to owning a fixed income product.

However, there are still a couple of choices to be made involving yields below 7%. Two possible scenarios to consider are the following:

1. A stock with a low dividend yield of 1.5% and less (which may go high as 2% plus), but with a fairly high dividend growth rate of around 10% to 12% per year, or
2. A stock with an average dividend yield of 2.5% to 5% (which may go as high 6% plus periodically) with an average dividend growth rate of around 5% to 8%.

I recommend that there is a place in one's portfolio for both, but my preference would be to hold a majority of stocks in your TFSA with a starting dividend yield of between 2.5% to 5%. Average-dividend yield stocks offer higher income from the start than low-yield stocks, and likely more sustainable dividend growth over time. This is especially true if the stock has a long history of growing the dividend at a reasonable rate, around 5% to 8%. For example, a stock with an initial dividend yield of 4%, which grows its dividend 5% per year, would have a yield of 7.92% after 15 years, which I feel is very reasonable. Low initial dividend yield, around 0.62% and growth of 15% per year would result in a 4.4% dividend yield after 15 years. Not a great yield after 15 years, but price growth may be higher.

Stocks with a low yield and high dividend growth usually do offer higher capital appreciation (the price of their shares growing), provided they can continue to maintain their high dividend growth rate (usually 10% and above) and might be best suited in a non-registered investment account. Two examples are the stocks MRU (Metro Inc) and CNR (Canadian National Railway). Let's look at these two:

CNR, as of this writing, has a current yield of 1.74%. It has a long and celebrated history of paying and growing their dividend, which began in 1995 when they were once a government-owned corporation.

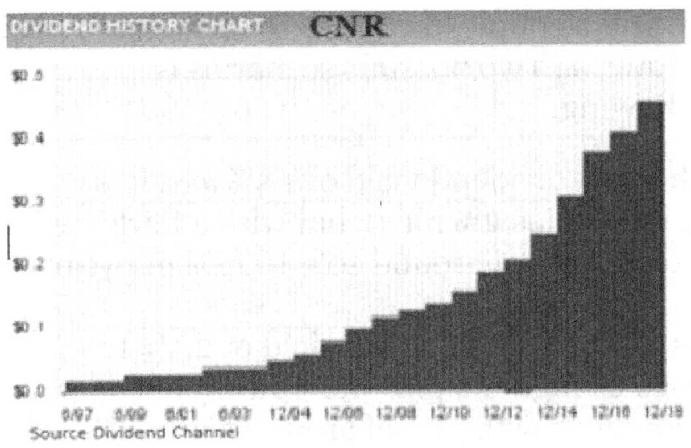

MRU, as of this writing, has a current yield of 1.38%, and it also has a long history of paying and growing their dividend.

Don't be misled by the chart below, as there was a dividend split.

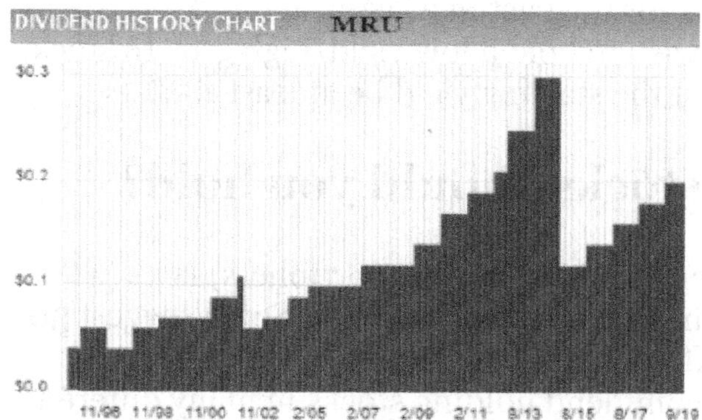

Notice how consistent the year-to-year dividend growth percentages are for the two stocks shown below:

CNR	2009	2010	2011	2012	2013	2014	2015	2016	2017	2018	Gth/Yld Ave
Dividend	0.51	0.54	0.65	0.75	0.86	1.00	1.25	1.50	1.65	1.82	256.86%
% Chg		5.88%	20.37%	15.38%	14.67%	16.28%	25.00%	20.00%	10.00%	10.30%	15.32%

MRU	2009	2010	2011	2012	2013	2014	2015	2016	2017	2018	Gth/Yld Ave
Dividend	0.18	0.22	0.25	0.28	0.32	0.38	0.45	0.54	0.63	0.70	288.89%
% Chg		22.22%	13.64%	12.00%	14.29%	18.75%	18.42%	20.00%	16.67%	11.11%	16.34%

Is one stock a better dividend payer than the other? You'll have to decide, or you could even pick both.

We can't predict the future growth rate of each stock, but we do have support for our assumptions every time they pay and raise their dividend. If the low-yield, high-growth company can maintain its high growth rate, then the stock will offer a higher total return than the average-yield stocks in the long run.

Back to the question of what the starting yield should be, especially for your TFSA account. I normally don't recommend a particular starting yield, but for your TFSA I suggest the following:

1. Select one of the stocks in your "List of Stocks to Consider" that offers a yield of 3.5% to 5.5%.

2. We'd like for the current yield to be above its 10-year average yield, but it isn't mandatory.
3. Its 10-year dividend growth rate should be over 75%.
4. The year-to-year dividend growth percentage should be above 5% for the past five years.
5. You might wish to hold a low yield/high growth stock, but I suggest the starting yield be at least 1.5%.

How many stocks should you hold?

The number of stocks to hold in your portfolio(s) is a personal choice, there is no magic number. Some suggest 30, 50 or even 100 different stocks or more for your entire portfolio. Most recommend holding stocks in many different sectors and markets to maximize diversification. Because I do not recommend vast diversification as a sound strategy for your income portfolio and especially for your TFSA, I would hope that you will not let others convince you to expand your holdings just to diversify.

If you are just beginning to invest in a TFSA, start with one or two stocks, from your "List of Stocks to Consider". Add more funds to your current stocks or add a new stock should you find one which offers a reasonable yield. Don't feel you need to immediately build up the number of holdings as quickly as possible. Rather, select stocks which will generate the most reliable income growth over the long-term. Remember we are seeking quality over quantity.

Personal Note: For my TFSA I owned one company stock for five years (2009-2014) before buying a second company stock. My wife owned only one stock for four years before adding a second company stock. I mentioned earlier that as of 2020 I still only hold four company stocks while my wife owns five company stocks in our TFSAs. One does not need to own a large number of company stocks to generate a good income from their TFSA, as I'll show in Chapter 5.

Price is not our main concern

Buy low and sell high is probably the most famous adage about trading in the stock market. What could be simpler? Unfortunately, it's only in hindsight that the lows and highs are recognized. At no point in time is it possible to predict the movement of a stock price. Some investors use a 50-day moving average or even a 200-day moving average. Many delve into the financial data of a business or even attempt to judge the mood of the market or market sentiment. Regardless of what subjective markers others try to use, it is always a challenge but not a concern for Income investors. Income investors have yield as their guide. A stock's current yield is determined by dividing a company's annual dividend by the current price. As mentioned earlier, you will then be able to compare the current yield to the 10-year average yield. This is your starting point.

So, price is important, but only in helping you determine the yield of a stock. The lower the price the higher the yield, but remember we are seeking a reasonable yield when considering to purchase. You should have set your yield range for the stocks on your list and will now monitor the stock price to see if you can purchase within the range you set. If the price is rising you may wish to adjust the yield range for a particular stock, or look to a different stock which may offer an acceptable yield.

Once you actually buy a stock, forget price, especially if the price continues to drop after purchasing. Should you have the money you may wish to buy more shares of the company, but don't feel bad if you don't get it at the lower price. Getting it at a reasonable yield was our goal, the price could just as easily have gone up.

Should there be a market correction likely all the stocks on your list will drop in price and this may be an opportunity to look at those stocks you always wanted to buy but were too expensive.

Let's consider some other methods of determining when a stock may offer a reasonable price.

Deciding upon a reasonable price or yield

Here are a few more simple methods to determine if the stock you wish to buy is value-priced (the price is low) and offers a good initial yield. You will be using the Excel worksheets again for your analysis:

1. I'll mention again to compare the current yield to the 10-year average yield. I'll use BCE as an example. The 10-year average yield is listed at the bottom right of the worksheet, shown as 4.96% in the chart below:

BCE	11-Dec-09	13-Dec-10	13-Dec-11	12-Dec-12	12-Dec-13	11-Dec-14	11-Dec-15	13-Dec-16	14-Dec-17	13-Dec-18	10 Yr Gth%
Dividend	1.58	1.79	2.05	2.22	2.33	2.47	2.60	2.73	2.87	3.02	**91.14%**
Div Gth Yld		13.04%	14.61%	8.55%	4.95%	6.00%	5.18%	5.08%	5.12%	5.15%	
Price	27.47	36.37	40.88	44.31	46.76	56.36	56.43	58.66	57.52	57.13	10y Ave Yld
Yield	5.75%	4.91%	5.01%	5.01%	4.99%	4.39%	4.61%	4.66%	4.99%	5.29%	**4.96%**
Current Yld	5.29%										

You will see that BCE's current yield is 5.29% which means that BCE is offering a higher yield than its average, which is good.

2. Another method is to compare the current price of the stock(s) to the 52-week low price. *The ca.Dividendinvestor.com* provides a quick way to view 52-week high/low price. Go to their website, http://ca.dividendinvestor.com/

Enter the stock's symbol: "BCE". Arrow down to:

ca.DividendInvestor.com

Stock Information	
Latest Close Price:	$ 57.75
52 Week Low - High:	$ 46.11 - $ 58.53
Revenue:	$ 2,051,000,000
Net Income:	$ 278,000,000
Cash Flow:	$ 857,000,000
EPS:	$ 0.64

Compare the current price of the stock(s) you are considering buying to its 52-week high and low price. If the current price is closer to the high price than the stock is probably too expensive, or at least has been rising over the 52-week period. If the price is closer to the lower price, than likely the price has dropped making it a better stock to consider purchasing. You can also compare the high/low range to the 10-year average yield of the stock you are considering.

4. For the third method, as recommended earlier, you will use the "Stk Consider" worksheet to project what the dividend yield would be if the current price drops.

10 Yr Ave Yield	Current Div	Current Price	Current Yield	Suggeste d Buy	Yield %	Suggeste d Buy	Yield %	Suggested Buy Price	Yield %
3.97%	3.48	$71.91	4.84%	$71.00	4.90%	$70.50	4.94%	$71.50	4.87%
4.94%	3.17	$63.37	5.00%	$63.00	5.03%	$62.50	5.07%	$64.00	4.95%

If the stock price drops you can quickly see what yield you would receive, the chart I have provided above shows the yield rises as the price decreases. The higher the yield the more income you will receive for each dollar invested. That's a good thing!

5. The fourth method uses the Adjusted Cost Base (ACB) or the "average cost" of your stocks. You can compare the current price of any stock you are considering buying to the ACB of the same stock you own. If the current price is close or lower than the ACB it may be a good time to buy. Calculating the ACB is not necessary with a TFSA, as it's tax-free, but you will see your average cost per share if you use my Excel worksheets to record your stocks' transactions, explained in Chapter 6.

6. Lastly, when you place your order with an online broker you can enter a "limit" price. This is the price you want to pay for the stock. The broker will not buy until the price reaches the price you set. You could intentionally enter a low price, around 10% below the current price, leave the bid open for a month or so and wait to see if the order gets filled.

Normally I recommend trying to buy when the price is low, but with a TFSA I suggest you try to contribute the maximum amount you can at the beginning of each year, even if you've reached your contribution limit. I want your TFSA money working as soon as possible, generating dividends, receiving dividend increases and allowing you to reinvest to generate even more income.

You can still look for a stock offering a reasonable yield whenever you choose, but by investing at the beginning of the year you can get your money working as quickly as possible within the TFSA. You may not be buying at the best price but you will be applying Dollar Cost Averaging, where you will buy more shares if the price is down and less when the price is up. I'd rather have your money collecting dividends sooner rather than later.

Note: When purchasing dividend stocks, you should be aware of the "Ex-dividend date". When the board announces a dividend for the next month or quarter, they also declare an ex-dividend date. Investors who purchased the stock before the **ex-dividend date** are entitled to the next **dividend** payment; those who purchased the stock on the **ex-dividend date** or after are not. Here's a website to obtain ex-dividend dates for companies of interest:

Farmer's 2019 TSX (Ex-)Dividend Listing   Dividends (TSX 60, ETF, REIT) ▾   Blogroll ▾

	Code	Company	Ex-Dividend Date	Payable Date	Yield	Frequency
		Preferred Shares Series A				
☑	BCE	BCE Inc.	Dec 13, 2019	Jan 15, 2020	4.95	Q

https://tsx.exdividend.ca/

Reinvested Dividends

With dividend-paying companies you have the choice of keeping the money (leaving it in your broker account) or using the cash dividend to buy more shares. Every time you use your dividends to buy more shares you increase your next dividend payment. If you reinvest again you buy even more shares and the cycle repeats itself. Dividend reinvestment is one of the most important parts of creating a compounding machine, your own *TFSA "Compounder"*.

Many investors prefer to let the dividends accumulate in their account and combine them with new funds for their next purchase. If you still maintained an un-contributed balance, this might be acceptable for your TFSA, but personally, I find this highly inefficient. What if you don't make the next purchase immediately or next month or even next quarter? Why not take advantage of commission-free reinvestment, even if only to ensure the regular accumulation of shares?

The three keys to enhanced compounding are: buying quality dividend growth stocks, buying

shares when they are value-priced and reinvesting the dividends.

This is the magic of compounding and I cannot emphasize enough its value as an Income investment tool. This also subscribes to my philosophy of "hands-off" investing, by utilizing automatic reinvesting it takes a lot of work off your shoulders. You are in the process of constantly acquiring shares, and those new shares will collect dividends and your dividends will become larger, and the cycle repeats.

***Reinvesting dividends along with dividend increases is what I mean by an ever-growing income!**

Canadian Investment Brokers

There are two methods of reinvesting dividends:

1. Synthetic dividend reinvestment allows the dividends received to purchase whole shares of the same company stock commission-free.
2. A company Dividend Reinvestment Plan (DRIP)is managed by a Transfer Agent and allows dividends to purchase whole and fractions of shares commission-free. Company DRIPs do not allow TFSA accounts so I will exclude DRIPs from this discussion.

	National Bank Direct Brokerage	Wealthsimple Trade	Questrade	Qtrade	RBC/TD/BMO/ CIBC/ScotiaB
Minimum Amount for No account fee	$20,000 across all accounts	No Minimum requirements	$1,000 across all accounts	$1,000 across all accounts	$15,000 to $25,000
Trading fees	$0.00	$0.00	$4.95	$8.75	$9.95
Automatic Dividend Reinvestment	Yes	No	Yes	Yes	Yes
Fractional share purchases	No	On Selected stocks	No	No	No
Trading Accounts offered	All types	TFSA, RRSP, and Single Non-registered	All types	All types	All types

Commission Free trading fees

National Bank Direct Brokerage and Wealthsimple Trade are currently the only two Canadian brokers offering commission free trading. Does it make a difference? Definitely! You now have the option of investing small amounts without being charged a fee. Previously, one would need to invest a minimum of $500 (with Questrade) to $1,000 (from most other brokers) to keep the commission fee at a 1% cost.

There are some key differences between the two commission free brokers:

National Bank:

1. Offers a full range of investing accounts, including TFSA, RRSP/RRIF, RESP, Non-registered (including Joint), and Pension accounts.
2. Offers automatic dividend reinvestment for full shares.
3. No fees to purchase US stocks.

Wealthsimple Trade:

1. Only offers TFSA, RRSP and single Non-registered accounts.
2. Does not have automatic dividend reinvestment.
3. Allows for fractions share purchase for selected Canadian stocks (currently about fifty).
4. Charges a 1.5% exchange fee on US stocks.

For Low-income earners, or those wishing to open just a TFSA account, I would consider Wealthsimple. Those wishing to invest in US stocks, should consider National Bank. Fractional shares do make a difference, because you'll be able to get every penny working to grow your income.

Here is a worksheet showing the dividends received from our TFSAs. See the slowly but continuously increasing amounts. or the totals for each account look at the amounts for every third month to see the growth.

Jan-19	Feb-19	Mar-19	Apr-19	May-19	Jun-19	Jul-19	Aug-19	Sep-19	Oct-19	Nov-19
198.87			211.59			214.36			217.19	
612.03			633.55			641.13			671.71	
		85.47			86.76			88.12		
107.34	149.22	149.96	150.93	151.91	152.92	153.98	154.99	155.98	156.86	157.86
918.24	149.22	235.43	996.07	151.91	239.68	1009.47	154.99	244.10	1045.76	157.86
198.87			211.59			214.36			217.19	
		87.90			88.69			89.45		
		85.47			86.76			88.12		
147.37	189.53	190.54	191.78	193.03	194.31	195.66	196.93	198.19	199.31	200.58
	493.04			498.16			526.47			532.36
346.24	682.57	363.91	403.37	691.19	369.76	410.02	723.40	375.76	416.50	732.94

Saving on a monthly basis and having the funds transferred to your TFSA account insures you'll be able to purchase shares on a regular basis. It is important to make saving a priority, and then to invest those savings as wisely as possible. And then leave those savings untouched, that is key to a sound retirement future. Consider these savings for retirement specifically, not to be touched until then!

Income investing is about growing your income gradually, not about making the big score. Find those quality dividend growth companies, buy your shares at a reasonable price, ones which offer a reasonable yield, reinvest the dividends, hopefully with full-dividend reinvestment receiving fractions of shares and add to your positions when you can. And by using the TFSA all monies accumulated through this process will be tax-free!

When to sell your TFSA stocks?

Regardless which account you have money invested, if you are investing for income and if you've selected quality dividend growth stocks for your portfolio, I believe you should consider them as your part-ownership in the business and never sell any of your shares. However, there are times when you should consider selling some or all of a company's shares, even in a TFSA:

- If the company cuts their dividend.
- If the company does not raise its dividend and you cannot justify holding the stock (it appears they will not raise it again soon).
- If you wish to shed stocks which have not performed as expected.
- If a major change effects the company (like a takeover) and you are more comfortable selling than waiting to see if the change is negative or positive.

I hope that you can see that you need to maintain the same scrutiny over your current roster of TFSA stocks that you applied when you first picked them. You should be monitoring the dividend payments, their increases, especially the dividend growth rates of all stocks you own. Don't panic if there is negative news regarding one of your holdings, certainly keep your eye on relevant activity, but as long as the monthly or quarterly dividends continue apace, and increase, there should be no reason to sell any of your stocks. The more information we have the better, but remember, we are not price-watching so we should not stress about the volatility of the market.

Chapter 4

The TFSA guidelines

This section is a summary of what I have discussed throughout the book.

1. Success in the future can only be attained if your own house is in order. Debt, especially high-interest debt will make others rich, not yourself.
2. Consider your TFSA as a retirement account, not a savings account. The money in your TFSA is intended to grow and meet your future needs not current ones.
3. Begin contributing to a TFSA as early as possible, increasing the amount you contribute, and maximizing your contribution limit as quickly as possible.
4. Once you have reached your maximum TFSA contribution limit, which includes under-contributed funds from previous years, you can only contribute the maximum allowed annually. There are penalties for over-contributing so be careful when making any additions to your account.
5. Don't forget to start a TFSA for your spouse, (even for your children over 18). Then you can double your annual contributions, or double whatever the allowable maximum is for that year.
6. Calculate the under-contributed amount for your spouse and try to meet their contribution limit as quickly as possible.
7. Select only quality dividend growth stocks to buy for your TFSA, after completing the Four-Rule Test and if they are on your "List of Stocks to Consider".
8. For your TFSA I do not recommend that you invest in:

- Fixed assets like GICs, Bonds, and Preferred stocks because we want a growing income, not a fixed one.
- High-yielding stocks (those with a yield above 7%),
- Mutual funds, ETFs and REITs because most will hold lower quality stocks or the income will be slow growth,
- Or any US dividend growth stocks in your TFSA because of withholding taxes.

9. Reinvest all dividends, hopefully with a Full Dividend Reinvestment Plan.

10. Add money to your existing holdings trying to contribute the maximum amount allowed for each year and reach your accumulated maximum as quickly as possible.

11. Only add a new company stock from your own list provided it meets your evaluation criteria.

12. Do not withdraw any of the TFSA funds for personal use, the money is for your retirement years.

13. Monitor your TFSA investments and record the transactions on the Excel worksheets, as we'll describe later in the book.

14. Do not sell any of your shares to take profits, to rebalance, only if there is a dividend cut.

15. Hold the stocks as long as they keep paying and growing your income. This will facilitate compounding.

16. Maximize your yearly TFSA and un-contributed limit before contributing to an RRSP or any other investment accounts. The exception would be a company RRSP sharing plan (never turn down free money).

Remember we are seeking to hold only quality dividend growth stocks and create a compounding machine which will produce a growing income and a rising yield on your investments. A TFSA is a perfect account for this kind of investing and saving. By growing the value of the account as much as we can, you'll reap such benefit when time comes for you to access the funds in your retirement, tax free! You'll see even more of this advantage when we get into the TFSA projections.

Buying shares and recording the TFSA transactions.

Once you have opened your TFSA account and evaluated your stocks you are ready to start purchasing stocks and tracking your transactions:

1. If you have opened your investment broker account, you can transfer the money you have to invest into your TFSA account.
2. Review your "List of Stocks to Consider" and decide which you might like to buy first.
3. Check the "Stks Consider" worksheet to see which stock(s) are currently offering a reasonable yield, or for the stock(s) you want to buy, in the sector you are considering.
4. If you have not entered the "Current Price" and "Suggested Prices" you can do so to check the range of yields available if you wish to buy immediately.

	List of Stocks to Consider			Start Div	Ending Div	10 Yr Div Gth%	10 Yr Ave Yield	Current Div	Current Price	Current Yield
1	Bank of Nova Scotia	BNS	Bank	1.96	3.28	67.35%	3.97%	0.48	$71.91	4.84%
2	BCE	BCE	Commun	1.58	3.02	91.14%	4.94%	0.17	$63.37	5.00%

5. Remember to consider the year-to-year dividend growth rate as well.
6. If you feel the price is acceptable, place your order to buy or you may set up a "Limit Order" at the price you'd like to buy at.
7. Once the stock is purchased, record the transaction in the "TFSA Stks" tab of your "Sample Reports Cdn New" worksheet.

8. Enter the stock Symbol you bought at the top left. I'll use BNS as my example:

BNS STOCK PURCHASES					BNS DIVIDEND RE-INVESTMENT			
Date	Price	Shares	Comm	Cost	Date	Price	Shares	Div Rec'd
				0.00	Jan 27\16	0.0000	0.0000	0.00
				0.00	Jan 27\16	0.0000	0.0000	0.00
				0.00	May 06\16	0.0000	0.0000	0.00
				0.00	Aug 05\16	0.0000	0.0000	0.00

9. Enter date, price paid, number of shares, including fractions and the commission paid on the left side.

BNS STOCK PURCHASES					BNS DIVIDEND RE-INVESTMENT				
Date	Price	Shares	Comm	Cost	Date	Price	Shares	Div Rec'd	Div
Sep 18\19	71.9100	20.8594	9.9500	1509.95	Nov 4\19	0.0000	0.0000	0.00	0.00
				0.00	Feb 9\20	0.0000	0.0000	0.00	

10. Next go to the "Summary" tab and you'll see this screen:

11. Notice that some of the information is already

SUMMARY REPORT								
TFSA Stocks	Total Invest	Org Shs	Div Shs	Total Shs	Av Cost	DIV	Yearly Div	Ave Yield
1st	$1,509.95	20.8594	0.0000	20.8594	$72.39	1.00	$20.86	1.38%

SUMMARY REPORT								
TFSA Stocks	Total Invest	Org Shs	Div Shs	Total Shs	Av Cost	DIV	Yearly Div	Ave Yield
BNS	$1,509.95	20.8594	0.0000	20.8594	$72.39	3.60	$75.09	4.97%
2nd	$0.00	0.0000	0.0000	0.0000	#DIV/0!	1.00	$0.00	#DIV/0!
3rd	$0.00	0.0000	0.0000	0.0000	#DIV/0!	1.00	$0.00	#DIV/0!
4th	$0.00	0.0000	0.0000	0.0000	#DIV/0!	1.00	$0.00	#DIV/0!
5th	$0.00	0.0000	0.0000	0.0000	#DIV/0!	1.00	$0.00	#DIV/0!
TFSA Total	$1,509.95	20.8594	0.0000	20.8594			$75.09	4.97%

showing on the first row. Type over "1st" with BNS and enter the current annual dividend, $3.60, being paid by BNS.

12. Guess what? You're done, at least until you receive your first dividend from BNS.

13. Then you'll go back to the "TFSA Stks" and record the dividend data on the right side. Here's an example:

BNS STOCK PURCHASES					BNS DIVIDEND RE-INVESTMENT				
Date	Price	Shares	Comm	Cost	Date	Price	Shares	Div Rec'd	Div
Sep 18\19	71.9100	20.8594	9.9500	1509.95	Nov 4\19	74.7809	0.2483	18.57	0.89
				0.00	Feb 9\20	0.0000	0.0000	0.00	

▸ ▸┃   /RRSP   TFSA Stks / Summary / Yld Proj / Div Gth / %Gth

SUMMARY REPORT

TFSA Stocks	Total Invest	Org Shs	Div Shs	Total Shs	Av Cost	DIV	Yearly Div	Ave Yield
BNS	$1,528.52	20.8594	0.2483	21.1077	$72.42	3.60	$75.99	4.97%
2nd	$0.00	0.0000	0.0000	0.0000	#DIV/0!	1.00	$0.00	#DIV/0!

▸ ▸┃   /RRSP / TFSA Stks / Summary / Yld Proj / Div Gth / %Gth

14. I've recorded fractions of shares for this example because the initial purchase was only $1,500, plus commission. Had we not been able to buy fractions of a share, the dividend of $18.57 would not be sufficient to buy a full share of BNS. You would then have to wait and add the funds to your next stock purchase.

15. Now you're done until you purchase a new stock or receive another dividend.

16. I've allowed for 10 company stocks in the "TFSA Stks" worksheet. If you require more, you can copy existing stock columns and paste them at the far right of the worksheet.

We'll discuss more about recording your investment transactions in Chapter 6.

Let's look at some TFSA projections

In the Disclaimer of this book I stated that your guess as to the future value of any security is as good as mine, or that of a broker. Forecasting is an unreliable enterprise.

I stand by that statement, and I will not be forecasting the future market value of your TFSA holdings, but rather the potential income your stocks might generate. Is there a difference? I believe so, because projecting income growth with my strategy is fairly easy and quite predictable.

De-mystifying compound growth:

Compound growth really is everything they say it is: magical, prodigious, and quite wondrous. But applying compound growth to future projections is often misleading.

Take the Rule of 72, which states that an interest rate will double when you divide it (the interest percentage) into 72. For example, if a stock (or your portfolio) offers a return of 9% a year, it should double in 8 years (72 / 9 = 8).Going from 9% to 18% in another 8 years may be possible, then from 18% to 36%, and so on, but perhaps too optimistic for our projection purposes.

Next let's look at the "start with a penny" phenomenon, which doubles the amount every day, giving you a whopping $5,368,709.12 after only 30 days.

Start with a penny and double the amount daily			
Day 1	$0.01	Day 16	$327.68
Day 2	$0.02	Day 17	$655.36
Day 3	$0.04	Day 18	$1,310.72
Day 4	$0.08	Day 19	$2,621.44
Day 5	$0.16	Day 20	$5,242.88
Day 6	$0.32	Day 21	$10,485.76
Day 7	$0.64	Day 22	$20,971.52
Day 8	$1.28	Day 23	$41,943.04
Day 9	$2.56	Day 24	$83,886.08
Day 10	$5.12	Day 25	$167,772.16
Day 11	$10.24	Day 26	$335,544.32
Day 12	$20.48	Day 27	$671,088.64
Day 13	$40.96	Day 28	$1,342,177.28
Day 14	$81.92	Day 29	$2,684,354.56
Day 15	$163.84	Day 30	$5,368,709.12

Unbelievable compounding for sure. However, if you look closely it takes 25 days for the value to reach $100,000, and then it's the last five days that provide 98.4% of the growth to achieve the $5,368,709.12.

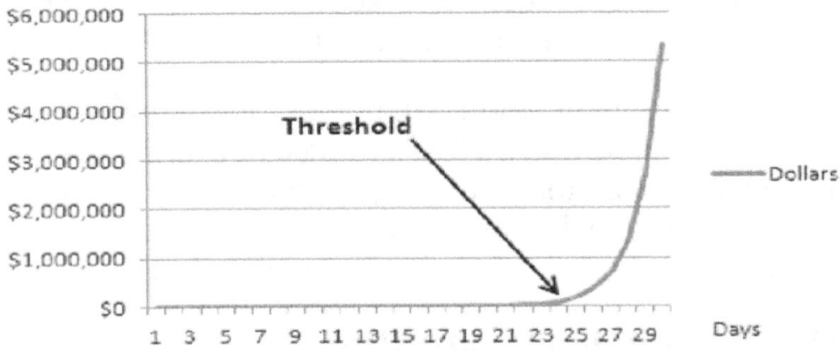

Projections like these might be fantastic, but the real difficulty with future financial projections is volatility! No one knows what the market movement, interest rates or even the dividend growth rates will be going forward. So, are all projections a waste of time? I don't think so because as an Income investor we can use past performance and investment results as a guide. Certainly, past performance is no guarantee that the future will duplicate the past, but Income investors do have an advantage others do not, **dividends and reinvested dividends**.

Even though markets and prices fluctuate, companies which have paid and raised their dividend consistently over a long period, 10 years and more, will very likely continue to do so into the future. So, if your dividends are essentially assured, your dividend reinvestments will always generate more income for your *TFSA "Compounder"*. Dividend reinvestment works in the opposite direction to what most believe. Everyone knows that when the market is down you purchase more shares with every dollar invested, in good times you purchase fewer shares. But regardless how the market reacts, you will automatically increase the number of shares you own and those new shares will generate a higher income to buy even more shares. Should the company(s) raise their dividend than all your current shares and any future shares of that company(s) would generate an even larger income than before. Besides reinvesting the dividends, when new funds are added to buy more shares, the income growth is accelerated.

I believe we can, with relative confidence, project one's future income growth, provided we stick with companies whose past history shows they have regularly and consistently paid and raised their dividend. Another nice part of the Income strategy is that you'll get confirmation your projections are on target each month or quarter when the companies announce the dividend or dividend increase.

The final key is to have reasonable expectations of your dividend growth, especially in the early years. Remember the chart which shows a penny doubling each day, the majority of the growth occurs at the end, rather than in the beginning.

As I've explained throughout the book, we'll be investing for income not capital appreciation. I expect the capital to grow, but there is no sure method to estimate future capital growth with any accuracy. Other books dealing with TFSAs will suggest investing for capital appreciation and most assume

TFSA 6 Percent Capital Growth

Annual Contributions	10 Years of 6% Growth	20 Years of 6% Growth	30 Years of 6% Growth	40 Years of 6% Growth
$1,000.00	$13,972.00	$38,993.00	$83,802.00	$164,048.00
$2,000.00	$27,943.00	$77,985.00	$167,603.00	$328,095.00
$3,000.00	$41,915.00	$116,978.00	$251,405.00	$492,143.00
$4,000.00	$55,887.00	$155,971.00	$335,207.00	$656,191.00
$5,000.00	$69,858.00	$194,964.00	$419,008.00	$820,238.00

your capital will grow by a constant percentage each year, say 6% or more each and every year. Stock market prices and compounding does not work that way and though you may average 6% or more capital growth over the long-term (actually 9%has been the long-term average), the actual results may look nothing like the projected figures. There is no reliable method of projecting capital appreciation. Here's an example of a typical capital appreciation forecast:

What I do agree with about capital projection, is that the more one invests and the longer they stay invested the greater the growth. The ideal situation would be for one to maximize their TFSA contribution limit immediately or as soon as possible. However, many are not in the position to contribute the maximum amounts allowed all at once and it may take many years before they can make up any under-contributed TFSA amounts. The key is to start investing in a TFSA as soon as possible and contribute as much as possible. Do not feel bad if it takes time for you to increase your investment and reach your contribution limit. Any time is the right time to begin to get the most from a TFSA.

When offering any projection, I think it is important to demonstrate a realistic scenario, one that encourages you to adopt my Income investment strategy at any age. But because I see such value in a TFSA, especially the earlier you begin, let's start with an 18 year old for this TFSA projection, using my "TFSA 18_60" worksheet. The chart below shows how much they should contribute over the years, from 18 thru to age 60, eventually reaching the maximum TFSA contributions allowed at age 55 and continuing to age 60. The estimated annual income each year is the highlighted column.

Age	Yearly Contributions	TFSA Max Contribution	Projected Annual Contribution	Balance of TFSA to Contribute	TFSA Total Invested Value	Projected Income Earned each Year	Projected Yield on Total Investment	Income % Inc each Year
18	$6,000.00	$6,000.00	$1,000.00	$5,000.00	$1,000.00	$40.00	4.00%	
19	$6,000.00	$12,000.00	$1,000.00	$10,000.00	$2,040.00	$83.64	4.10%	109.10%
20	$6,000.00	$18,000.00	$1,000.00	$15,000.00	$3,123.64	$131.19	4.20%	56.85%
21	$6,000.00	$24,000.00	$1,000.00	$20,000.00	$4,254.83	$182.96	4.30%	39.46%
22	$6,000.00	$30,000.00	$1,000.00	$25,000.00	$5,437.79	$239.26	4.40%	30.77%
23	$6,000.00	$36,000.00	$1,000.00	$30,000.00	$6,677.05	$300.47	4.50%	25.58%
24	$6,000.00	$42,000.00	$1,000.00	$35,000.00	$7,977.52	$366.97	4.60%	22.13%
25	$6,000.00	$48,000.00	$3,000.00	$38,000.00	$11,344.49	$533.19	4.70%	45.30%
26	$6,000.00	$54,000.00	$3,000.00	$41,000.00	$14,877.68	$714.13	4.80%	33.93%
27	$6,000.00	$60,000.00	$3,000.00	$44,000.00	$18,591.81	$911.00	4.90%	27.57%
28	$6,000.00	$66,000.00	$3,000.00	$47,000.00	$22,502.80	$1,125.14	5.00%	23.51%
29	$6,000.00	$72,000.00	$3,000.00	$50,000.00	$26,627.95	$1,358.03	5.10%	20.70%
30	$6,000.00	$78,000.00	$6,000.00	$50,000.00	$33,985.97	$1,767.27	5.20%	30.14%
31	$6,000.00	$84,000.00	$6,000.00	$50,000.00	$41,753.24	$2,212.92	5.30%	25.22%
32	$6,000.00	$90,000.00	$6,000.00	$50,000.00	$49,966.16	$2,698.17	5.40%	21.93%
33	$6,000.00	$96,000.00	$6,000.00	$50,000.00	$58,664.34	$3,226.54	5.50%	19.58%
34	$6,000.00	$102,000.00	$6,000.00	$50,000.00	$67,890.87	$3,801.89	5.60%	17.83%
35	$6,000.00	$108,000.00	$6,000.00	$50,000.00	$77,692.76	$4,428.49	5.70%	16.48%
36	$6,000.00	$114,000.00	$6,000.00	$50,000.00	$88,121.25	$5,111.03	5.80%	15.41%
37	$6,000.00	$120,000.00	$6,000.00	$50,000.00	$99,232.28	$5,854.70	5.90%	14.55%
38	$6,000.00	$126,000.00	$6,000.00	$50,000.00	$111,086.99	$6,665.22	6.00%	13.84%
39	$6,000.00	$132,000.00	$6,000.00	$50,000.00	$123,752.21	$7,548.88	6.10%	13.26%
40	$6,000.00	$138,000.00	$8,000.00	$48,000.00	$139,301.09	$8,636.67	6.20%	14.41%
41	$6,000.00	$144,000.00	$8,000.00	$46,000.00	$155,937.76	$9,824.08	6.30%	13.75%
42	$6,000.00	$150,000.00	$8,000.00	$44,000.00	$173,761.84	$11,120.76	6.40%	13.20%
43	$6,000.00	$156,000.00	$8,000.00	$42,000.00	$192,882.60	$12,537.37	6.50%	12.74%
44	$6,000.00	$162,000.00	$8,000.00	$40,000.00	$213,419.96	$14,085.72	6.60%	12.35%
45	$6,000.00	$168,000.00	$8,000.00	$38,000.00	$235,505.68	$15,778.88	6.70%	12.02%
46	$6,000.00	$174,000.00	$10,000.00	$34,000.00	$261,284.56	$17,767.35	6.80%	12.60%
47	$6,000.00	$180,000.00	$10,000.00	$30,000.00	$289,051.91	$19,944.58	6.90%	12.25%
48	$6,000.00	$186,000.00	$10,000.00	$26,000.00	$318,996.49	$22,329.75	7.00%	11.96%
49	$6,000.00	$192,000.00	$10,000.00	$22,000.00	$351,326.25	$24,944.16	7.10%	11.71%
50	$6,000.00	$198,000.00	$10,000.00	$18,000.00	$386,270.41	$27,811.47	7.20%	11.49%
51	$6,000.00	$204,000.00	$10,000.00	$14,000.00	$424,081.88	$30,957.98	7.30%	11.31%
52	$6,000.00	$210,000.00	$10,000.00	$10,000.00	$465,039.86	$34,412.95	7.40%	11.16%
53	$6,000.00	$216,000.00	$10,000.00	$6,000.00	$509,452.81	$38,208.96	7.50%	11.03%
54	$6,000.00	$222,000.00	$10,000.00	$2,000.00	$557,661.77	$42,382.29	7.60%	10.92%
55	$6,000.00	$228,000.00	$8,000.00	$0.00	$608,044.06	$46,819.39	7.70%	10.47%
56	$6,000.00	$234,000.00	$6,000.00	$0.00	$660,863.46	$51,547.35	7.80%	10.10%
57	$6,000.00	$240,000.00	$6,000.00	$0.00	$718,410.81	$56,754.45	7.90%	10.10%
58	$6,000.00	$246,000.00	$6,000.00	$0.00	$781,165.26	$62,493.22	8.00%	10.11%
59	$6,000.00	$252,000.00	$6,000.00	$0.00	$849,658.48	$68,822.34	8.10%	10.13%
60	$6,000.00	$258,000.00	$6,000.00	$0.00	$924,480.82	$75,807.43	8.20%	10.15%

If you review the above chart, you will notice the dividing line at age 38. At that age I've projected the person has invested $76,000, from age 18 to 38 (the sum of their Projected Annual Contribution), and would be receiving $6,665.22 of income per year from their investment. The income is growing slowly but steadily and if you look at the "Projected Yield on Total Investment" column, you will see that the yield also grows steadily each year.

Now if you look 10 years ahead, to age 48, you will see that the annual income is projected at $$22,329.75, a 235% increase over age 38. From age 48 onward the income growth continues to accelerate even faster.

Beginning a TFSA at 18 years old

Will an 18 year old have enough money to begin investing $1,000 per year in a TFSA, let alone increase the amounts as suggested? Unlikely, but what if, we instead ask how many 18 year olds have a new iPhone or the latest computer, or the latest gadget? Don't those items often cost around $1,000? If people are willing to pay that kind of money for such luxury items, why couldn't a savings account be given the same priority? Are there parents out there willing to help their child get a jump start on saving by opening a TFSA and assisting with contributions? These parents will be doing their child(ren) a great service impressing upon them the importance of a TFSA and why they should continue to contribute on their own once they begin earning their own income.

Better yet consider starting a company Dividend Reinvestment Plan (DRIP) for your child(ren), as soon as you can. I explained DRIPs in my first book *Your Ever Growing Income: The Rising Yield on Investments*. If you start a DRIP for a minor it would be a joint account with an adult and the adult would claim the dividend income as taxable, not the minor. Once the child is 18 the DRIP would be transferred to the child's name and the dividends would be claimed as taxable income to them. But should the child's taxable income be less than $45,000 per year no tax would be payable on the dividends. The advantage of keeping the DRIP open after age 18 and until they begin to earn their own income, is that there will be no commissions to buy and reinvest shares, they can continue to invest small amounts and of course they will buy fractions of shares.

I recommend they open a TFSA once they begin to earn income to be able to contribute$1,000 or more to a TFSA. At that stage the DRIP would have served its purpose and could be closed.

By keeping the child aware of the DRIP and showing them how their income grows each and every year, will help them recognize its advantages and encourage them to continue investing. It is such a valuable gift to offer your children, a head start on savings in an investment vehicle that takes full advantage of compounding.

The worksheet projections for an 18 year old assumes the following:

1. You are 18 as of 2020.
2. You can begin investing $1,000 per year.
3. Your contributions should increase over time with the expectation that you will not meet your maximum contributions (making up the under-contributions) until age 55. This will change if you increase or decrease the amounts you invest.
4. The starting yield of your investments will be 4% (which is reasonable in 2020).
5. I've left the maximum annual contributions fixed at $6,000 per year.
6. I'm assuming there will be no major changes to the TFSA contribution guidelines by CRA.

When you review the chart for the 18 year old (or any of the other TFSA age Excel worksheets), one of the key items to watch is the "Yield on Total Investment" column. The percentage rises slowly and steadily. That is the rising yield from your dividend growth investments and will be one of the measurements which confirms that your income is growing.

Income investing in a TFSA must be considered a long-term strategy, but the results will be worth your effort and patience. You won't get the same income growth results with other investments. For example, take a look at these three Canadian ETFs. The bold items are distribution decreases.

VDY

Jan-00	Jan-00	Jan-00	Jan-00	Dec-13	Dec-14	Dec-15	Jan-17	Dec-17	Dec-18	10 Yr Gth%
0.00	0.00	0.00	0.00	0.75	1.32	1.12	1.02	1.33	1.33	**76.10%**
	#DIV/0!	#DIV/0!	#DIV/0!	#DIV/0!	75.83%	**-15.56%**	**-8.86%**	30.23%	**0.00%**	

XEI

Jan-00	Jan-00	Jan-00	Dec-12	Dec-13	Dec-14	Dec-15	Dec-16	Dec-17	Dec-18	10 Yr Gth%
0.00	0.00	0.00	0.85	0.96	0.98	1.01	0.97	0.96	1.03	**21.70%**
	#DIV/0!	#DIV/0!	#DIV/0!	12.97%	2.09%	3.37%	**-4.45%**	**-0.31%**	7.17%	

ZDV

Jan-00	Jan-00	Jan-00	Dec-12	Jan-14	Jan-15	Jan-16	Dec-16	Dec-17	Dec-18	10 Yr Gth%
0.00	0.00	0.00	0.57	0.82	0.75	0.72	0.77	0.76	0.82	**43.36%**
	#DIV/0!	#DIV/0!	#DIV/0!	44.06%	**-8.98%**	**-4.00%**	6.25%	**-1.18%**	8.47%	

It's not high yield you should seek, but a steady and continuous income growth from your investments.

I have also setup worksheets and projections for those starting at a later age than 18. Here is the schedule of the minimum starting annual contributions I used in my projections, dependent upon the age you start a TFSA:

18 to 24 $1,000 per year
25 to 29 $3,000 per year
30 to 39 $6,000 per year
40 to 45 $8,000 per year
46 to 55 $10,000 per year
55 and over $6,000 per year (as you've probably reached the maximum contribution limit).

There are also blank TFSA worksheets for yourself and a spouse to enter your actual TFSA contributions to date and project them into the future.

Earning $45,000 at age 34?

I've suggested investing in a TFSA before contributing to an RRSP. Industry advice, almost across the board tends to suggest the opposite. I do believe all parties would agree that one should contribute the maximum amount to both accounts, if possible, to receive the most benefit from your investments.

However, I do believe if one follows the strategy of maximizing their TFSA first, then contribute any additional funds into an RRSP, it is very likely that when one retires, one will live very comfortably and pay hardly any taxes.

To illustrate my position, let's consider a 34 year old who earns $45,000 per year. I will also make a few other assumptions:

1. They expect that their salary will increase at a rate of 3% per year.
2. As of age 34 they have contributed $33,000 towards a TFSA and no funds into an RRSP.
3. They will expect to be able to contribute $4,000 per year into their TFSA and gradually increase the amount as shown on the following chart.
4. They will not contribute to a RRSP unless they can reach their TFSA maximum contributed amount, which they should reach at age 50 following our estimate of annual contributions.
5. Should they reach their TFSA limit sooner they will then contribute to an RRSP.

Here's a summary of their potential TFSA income from age 34 to 55.

Age	Salary	Max RRSP Cont. 18%	Yearly TFSA Max Contributions	Funds Available after TFSA	TFSA Max Contribution	Actual Annual Contribution	Balance of TFSA to Contribute	TFSA Total Invested Value	Projected Annual Income
34	$45,000				$63,500	$33,000	$30,500	$33,000	$1,749
35	$46,350	$8,343	$6,000.00	$2,343	$69,500	$4,000	$32,500	$38,749	$2,131
36	$47,741	$8,593	$6,000.00	$2,593	$75,500	$4,000	$34,500	$44,880	$2,558
37	$49,173	$8,851	$6,000.00	$2,851	$81,500	$4,000	$36,500	$51,438	$3,035
38	$50,648	$9,117	$6,000.00	$3,117	$87,500	$6,000	$36,500	$60,473	$3,689
39	$52,167	$9,390	$6,000.00	$3,390	$93,500	$6,000	$36,500	$70,162	$4,420
40	$53,732	$9,672	$6,000.00	$3,672	$99,500	$7,500	$35,000	$82,082	$5,335
41	$55,344	$9,962	$6,000.00	$3,962	$105,500	$7,500	$33,500	$94,918	$6,359
42	$57,005	$10,261	$6,000.00	$4,261	$111,500	$7,500	$32,000	$108,777	$7,506
43	$58,715	$10,569	$6,000.00	$4,569	$117,500	$7,500	$30,500	$123,783	$8,789
44	$60,476	$10,886	$6,000.00	$4,886	$123,500	$7,500	$29,000	$140,071	$10,225
45	$62,291	$11,212	$6,000.00	$5,212	$129,500	$10,000	$25,000	$160,297	$12,022
46	$64,159	$11,549	$6,000.00	$5,549	$135,500	$10,000	$21,000	$182,319	$14,039
47	$66,084	$11,895	$6,000.00	$5,895	$141,500	$10,000	$17,000	$206,357	$16,302
48	$68,067	$12,252	$6,000.00	$6,252	$147,500	$10,000	$13,000	$232,660	$18,845
49	$70,109	$12,620	$6,000.00	$6,620	$153,500	$10,000	$9,000	$261,505	$21,705
50	$72,212	$12,998	$6,000.00	$6,998	$159,500	$10,000	$5,000	$293,210	$24,923
51	$74,378	$13,388	$6,000.00	$7,388	$165,500	$10,000	$1,000	$328,133	$28,548
52	$76,609	$13,790	$6,000.00	$7,790	$171,500	$7,000	$0	$363,680	$32,368
53	$78,908	$14,203	$6,000.00	$8,203	$177,500	$6,000	$0	$402,048	$36,586
54	$81,275	$14,630	$6,000.00	$8,630	$183,500	$6,000	$0	$444,634	$41,351
55	$83,713	$15,068	$6,000.00	$9,068	$189,500	$6,000	$0	$491,985	$46,739

Assuming the income projections are reasonable, they can expect their TFSA to provide approximately $46,739 of tax-free income by the age of 55. Remember we have not included any spousal TFSA investment in this scenario, which could considerably increase their tax-free income.

How about a married 40 year old with two kids?

I'll assume that both the husband (age 40) and wife (age 38) in this projection are working and their combined income is some where between $100,000 and $120,000 per year. I won't estimate their expenses but will assume they both started a TFSA in 2009.Let's say he has contributed $34,000 and she contributes $25,000 by2019, leaving both with un-contributed TFSA balances. Beginning in 2020 they can afford to put aside $10,000 per year ($6,000 in his and $4,000 in hers). By age 45 they will increase their savings to $15,000 per year and $20,000 by age 50, allowing them to eventually reach the maximum allowable TFSA contributions by age 54 and 59 respectively. Here's their potential tax-free income projection.

His Age	Combined Amount Invested	Combined Annual Income
40	$59,000.00	$2,997.12
45	$77,000.00	$7,767.92
50	$123,000.00	$17,693.01
55	$169,500.00	$36,529.71
60	$199,500.00	$68,486.88
65	$229,500.00	$122,650.60

These examples show that even if you are unable to max out your un-contributed TFSA funds till later in life, you will know as the years pass (monthly and quarterly) if your income is growing at a reasonable rate and if your end goal is then achievable. Because we cannot look into the future, we must instead make assumptions. And because I would rather provide a more realistic scenario, I believe you will find both the income and yield projections on the low side. But even as a conservative estimate, I hope you feel excited about the potential for quite a comfortable income at retirement.

Remember, market volatility is your companion to achieving a higher income and yields, not a hindrance. Don't get caught up in the headlines or suggestions that there is possible doom and gloom ahead, instead welcome them.

Let's check my projections

Here's a portion of the 18 year old's projection. Look at the highlighted areas on the chart. It shows an invested amount of $14,879.03 with income of $714.19 and a yield of 4.80%.

Age	TFSA Max Contribution	Projected Annual Contribution	Balance of TFSA to Contribute	TFSA Total Invested Value	Income Earned each Year	Yield on Investment
18	$6,000.00	$1,000.00	$5,000.00	$1,000.00	$41.00	4.10%
19	$12,000.00	$1,000.00	$10,000.00	$2,041.00	$83.68	4.10%
20	$18,000.00	$1,000.00	$15,000.00	$3,124.68	$131.24	4.20%
21	$24,000.00	$1,000.00	$20,000.00	$4,255.92	$183.00	4.30%
22	$30,000.00	$1,000.00	$25,000.00	$5,438.92	$239.31	4.40%
23	$36,000.00	$1,000.00	$30,000.00	$6,678.23	$300.52	4.50%
24	$42,000.00	$1,000.00	$35,000.00	$7,978.76	$367.02	4.60%
25	$48,000.00	$3,000.00	$38,000.00	$11,345.78	$533.25	4.70%
26	$54,000.00	$3,000.00	$41,000.00	$14,879.03	$714.19	4.80%

Now look at an actual dividend growth investment account where the highlighted area shows an invested amount of $13,467.66 with income of $767.36 and a yield of 5.70%.

Year	Invested amount	Dividend income by Year	Dividend % growth each Year	Original Investment plus Dividends	Accumulated investment	Yield on Investment
2007	$5,555.00	$0.00		$5,555.00	$5,555.00	
2008	$500.00	$217.80		$717.80	$6,272.80	
2009	$500.00	$253.81	16.53%	$753.81	$7,026.61	3.61%
2010	$0.00	$281.43	10.88%	$281.43	$7,308.04	3.85%
2011	$1,000.00	$323.94	15.10%	$1,323.94	$8,631.98	3.75%
2012	$0.00	$379.31	17.09%	$379.31	$9,011.29	4.21%
2013	$0.00	$431.66	13.80%	$431.66	$9,442.95	4.57%
2014	$0.00	$481.32	11.50%	$481.32	$9,924.27	4.85%
2015	$0.00	$531.84	10.50%	$531.84	$10,456.11	5.09%
2016	$0.00	$588.67	10.69%	$588.67	$11,044.78	5.33%
2017	$1,000.00	$655.52	11.36%	$1,655.52	$12,700.30	5.16%
2018	$0.00	$767.36	17.06%	$767.36	$13,467.66	5.70%

With our 18 year old's projection we are estimating less income ($714.19 compared to $767.36) with more money invested. With a higher amount invested we should get more income, but we are keeping our projection on the low side.

Now let's compare our 18 year old's TFSA projection to two actual TFSA accounts, looking at larger amounts invested. The highlighted area, for the 18 year old, shows a total

Age	TFSA Max Contribution	Projected Annual Contribution	Balance of TFSA to Contribute	TFSA Total Invested Value	Income Earned each Year	Yield on Investment
18	$6,000.00	$1,000.00	$5,000.00	$1,000.00	$41.00	4.10%
19	$12,000.00	$1,000.00	$10,000.00	$2,041.00	$83.68	4.10%
20	$18,000.00	$1,000.00	$15,000.00	$3,124.68	$131.24	4.20%
21	$24,000.00	$1,000.00	$20,000.00	$4,255.92	$183.00	4.30%
22	$30,000.00	$1,000.00	$25,000.00	$5,438.92	$239.31	4.40%
23	$36,000.00	$1,000.00	$30,000.00	$6,678.23	$300.52	4.50%
24	$42,000.00	$1,000.00	$35,000.00	$7,978.76	$367.02	4.60%
25	$48,000.00	$3,000.00	$38,000.00	$11,345.78	$533.25	4.70%
26	$54,000.00	$3,000.00	$41,000.00	$14,879.03	$714.19	4.80%
27	$60,000.00	$3,000.00	$44,000.00	$18,593.22	$911.07	4.90%
28	$66,000.00	$3,000.00	$47,000.00	$22,504.29	$1,125.21	5.00%
29	$72,000.00	$3,000.00	$50,000.00	$26,629.51	$1,358.10	5.10%
30	$78,000.00	$6,000.00	$50,000.00	$33,987.61	$1,767.36	5.20%
31	$84,000.00	$6,000.00	$50,000.00	$41,754.97	$2,213.01	5.30%
32	$90,000.00	$6,000.00	$50,000.00	$49,967.98	$2,698.27	5.40%
33	$96,000.00	$6,000.00	$50,000.00	$58,666.25	$3,226.64	5.50%
34	$102,000.00	$6,000.00	$50,000.00	$67,892.89	$3,802.00	5.60%
35	$108,000.00	$6,000.00	$50,000.00	$77,694.90	$4,428.61	5.70%

investment of $77,694.90 and a projected income of $4,428.61 with a yield of 5.70%.

The next two charts are actual TFSA accounts with approximately the same total invested amounts. Compare these to the 18 year old's projected income of $4,428.61 and yield of 5.70%.

Year	Maximum Contribution by Year	Dividend income by Year	Dividend % growth each Year	Original Investment plus Dividends	Accumulated investment	Yield on Investment
2009	5,000.00	144.94		5,144.94	5,144.94	2.82%
2010	5,000.00	399.00	175.29%	5,399.00	10,543.94	3.78%
2011	5,000.00	862.35	116.13%	5,862.35	16,406.29	5.26%
2012	5,000.00	959.70	11.29%	5,959.70	22,365.99	4.29%
2013	5,500.00	1313.46	36.86%	6,813.46	29,179.45	4.50%
2014	5,500.00	1742.35	32.65%	7,242.35	36,421.80	4.78%
2015	10,000.00	2404.75	38.02%	12,404.75	48,826.55	4.93%
2016	5,500.00	3301.78	37.30%	8,801.78	57,628.33	5.73%
2017	5,500.00	3813.66	15.50%	9,313.66	66,941.99	5.70%
2018	5,500.00	4574.95	19.96%	10,074.95	77,016.94	5.94%
2019	6,000.00	5432.10	18.74%	11,432.10	88,449.04	6.14%

Year	Maximum Contribution by Year	Dividend income by Year	Dividend % growth each Year	Original Investment plus Dividends	Accumulated investment	Yield on Investment
2009	5,000.00	129.82		5,129.82	5,129.82	2.53%
2010	5,000.00	399.00	207.35%	5,399.00	10,528.82	3.79%
2011	5,000.00	758.17	90.02%	5,758.17	16,286.99	4.66%
2012	5,000.00	1,116.20	47.22%	6,116.20	22,403.19	4.98%
2013	5,500.00	1,516.00	35.82%	7,016.00	29,419.19	5.15%
2014	5,500.00	2,182.03	43.93%	7,682.03	37,101.22	5.88%
2015	10,000.00	2,917.74	33.72%	12,917.74	50,018.96	5.83%
2016	5,500.00	3,661.32	25.48%	9,161.32	59,180.28	6.19%
2017	5,500.00	4,143.28	13.16%	9,643.28	68,823.56	6.02%
2018	5,500.00	5,060.57	22.14%	10,560.57	79,384.13	6.37%
2019	6,000.00	5,646.90	11.59%	11,646.90	91,031.03	6.20%

These two TFSA accounts belong to me and my wife. Our total invested amounts are $77,016.94 and $79,384.13. These are not market value figures but our maximum TFSA contributions plus the reinvested dividends.

Our income shows $4,574.95 and $5,060.57 with yields of 5.94% and 6.37% respectively. But both of our incomes and yields are higher than the 18 year old's projection with roughly the same amounts invested (my wife's is slightly higher, but has a much higher yield), showing again that my projection for the 18 year old's income is on the conservative side. Also note that we invested higher amounts in 10 years than the 18 year old did in 18 years. This reinforces the statement that the more one saves and invests the quicker your income will grow.

Talk is cheap!

At this point I would like to take the opportunity to bring up an important point about disposable income and savings. I do not want to sugarcoat the process I'm suggesting. I've stressed the importance of saving and making the TFSA your number one retirement savings account. I've also talked a lot about how much one needs to save to meet their future needs, but we haven't discussed just where exactly this money comes from. According to many studies it's becoming more difficult for individuals and families to save because a larger portion of their disposable income is going towards

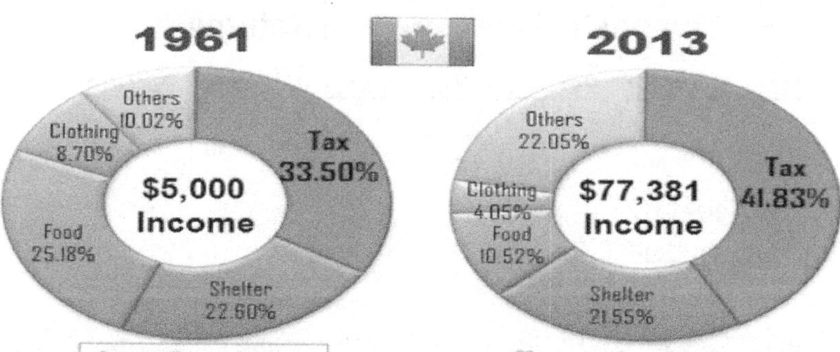

taxes.

Because more of your income is being paid towards taxes, it means your disposable income is shrinking, and you must either cut expenses in other areas or find ways to increase your income if you wish to put aside enough money to save for your retirement needs. This makes it imperative that the money you do save generate as much income as possible, making *Your TFSA Compounder* that much more valuable to your retirement savings strategy!

Let's step back a minute

Now that you've seen some of my projections, you might be saying: "Aren't you projecting and doing exactly what everyone else does? They project a 6% or 7% capital increase every year while you project a 0.02% rising yield each year"?

Yes, but I also believe the steadily rising yield can be justified and I'll explain why. First, let me dispel the capital projection. We know that market returns will be positive and negative going forward, never a fixed or constant growing return. The big problem is we don't know how severe the negative returns will be or how high the positive, or how long each will last. It's simply impossible to know or predict. Let's look at the annual returns of the TSX Composite Index for 19

TSX Composite Index: Annual Returns

Year	Percent	Year	Percent	Year	Percent	Year	Percent
2000	1.7	2006	17.4	2012	4.0	2018	-11.6
2001	-12.2	2007	7.8	2013	9.6		
2002	-12.8	2008	-35.5	2014	7.4		
2003	19.3	2009	30.7	2015	-11.1		
2004	13.9	2010	14.4	2016	17.5		
2005	22.9	2011	-11.1	2017	6.0		

The annual gain or loss in the TSX Composite index from 2000 to present. Dividends are not included.

years from 2000 to 2018 and show it as a bar chart.

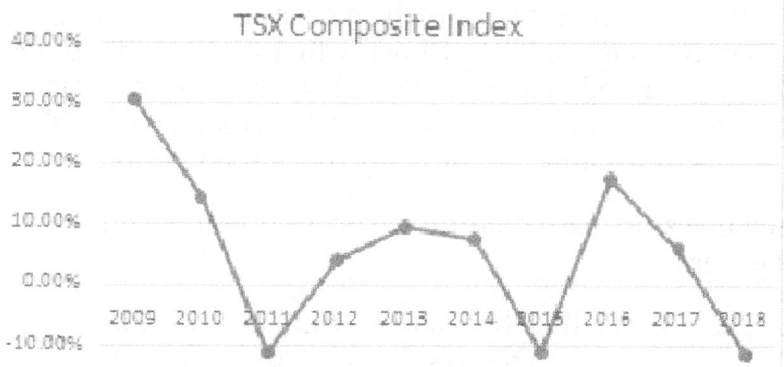

Earlier in this chapter I presented the chart below, where others have projected capital growth for your TFSA investments using annual returns of 6% per year:

TFSA 6 Percent Capital Growth

Annual Contributions	10 Years of 6% Growth	20 Years of 6% Growth	30 Years of 6% Growth	40 Years of 6% Growth
$1,000.00	$13,972.00	$38,993.00	$83,802.00	$164,048.00
$2,000.00	$27,943.00	$77,985.00	$167,603.00	$328,095.00
$3,000.00	$41,915.00	$116,978.00	$251,405.00	$492,143.00
$4,000.00	$55,887.00	$155,971.00	$335,207.00	$656,191.00
$5,000.00	$69,858.00	$194,964.00	$419,008.00	$820,238.00

If I apply the actual TSX Composite returns for the past 19 years, from 2000 to 2018 here's how the capital would have actually grown, when compared to the above projected 6%:

TSX Composite Actual Returns 2000 to 2018

Annual Contributions	20 Years of Actual Growth	20 Years of 6% Growth	Difference
$1,000.00	$25,449.55	$38,993.00	-$13,543.45
$2,000.00	$50,899.10	$77,985.00	-$27,085.90
$3,000.00	$76,348.65	$116,978.00	-$40,629.35
$4,000.00	$101,798.20	$155,971.00	-$54,172.80
$5,000.00	$127,247.75	$194,964.00	-$67,716.25

There are gains but in no way do they match the projected figures. And who knows what the next 20 years will hold for the markets. Projecting capital growth at a fixed rate of return is a tricky business. One might do better or worse during the next 20 years, it's really a guessing game and I would not be comfortable putting my financial security in the hands of an unpredictable and volatile market. No one can foresee where the market will go; only by looking back will you be able to see how well or badly the market performed.

Income investors base their future projections on a different set of criteria:

1. We take the time to evaluate companies over a long time-period and try to select only those companies which have continued to be successful, despite difficult times. We choose companies which have shown that they can adjust to and weather the changes in the economy and market sentiment.
2. We concentrate on companies that continue to generate positive earnings and pass along a portion of those earning to their shareholders.
3. When making stock purchases Income investors seek to obtain a reasonable yield, usually higher than the average yield of the stock over a 10 year period.
4. Income investors take a different view of fluctuations in the market. We not only assume there will be market changes over the next twenty or thirty years, we welcome them.
5. What everyone else fears we count on! When times are unstable and the market is going down your stock purchases and dividend reinvestments will provide higher yields. Higher yield on purchases mean higher income.
6. When times are good and the market is rising, your purchases will provide lower yields. But during good times it is more likely that quality companies will increase their dividend which will offset the lower yield of higher prices.
7. More importantly, those dividend increases will increase the yield on all your earlier purchases, especially those bought during down markets.

In short, Income investors are in a win-win situation, regardless if the market is soaring or in crisis. Your yield on investment and income should increase slowly and steadily. That's why my yield projection increases are reasonable and relevant.

There is a Chinese proverb which says "one picture is worth ten thousand words". So, let's look at a chart of me and my wife's actual TFSA income growth from 2009 to 2019 (which includes the financial crisis). As of 2019 our combined income will be just under $12,000 with an investment of $179,601.35 (includes reinvested dividends), and a yield of 6.18%:

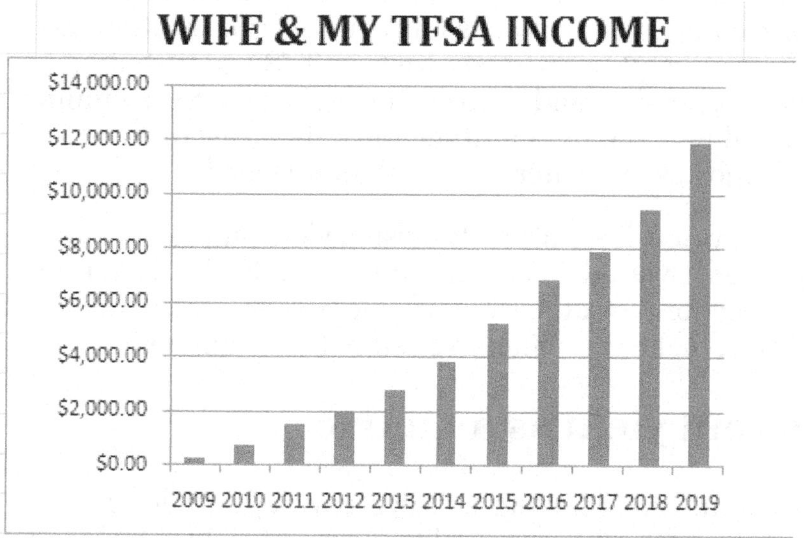

With the steady income growth shown in this chart, our yield on total investment also rises. Look at our combined actual Yield on Investment since we started our TFSAs in 2009.

	Original invest	Our Yearly Div Income	Total with Div Reinvest	Yield on Investment
2009	$10,000.00	$274.76	$10,274.76	2.67%
2010	$10,000.00	$775.77	$21,072.76	3.79%
2011	$10,000.00	$1,570.52	$32,693.28	4.96%
2012	$10,000.00	$2,025.90	$44,769.18	4.64%
2013	$11,000.00	$2,779.46	$58,598.64	4.83%
2014	$11,000.00	$3,874.38	$73,523.02	5.33%
2015	$20,000.00	$5,272.49	$98,845.51	5.38%
2016	$11,000.00	$6,863.10	$116,808.61	5.96%
2017	$11,000.00	$7,906.94	$135,765.55	5.86%
2018	$11,000.00	$9,441.52	$156,506.17	6.22%
2019	$12,000.00	$11,890.47	$179,601.35	6.18%

You too can achieve similar results to ours by following my Income investment strategy. Stick with quality dividend growth companies. Invest as much as you can, as often as you can, attempting to maximize your TFSA contributions as quickly as possible and reinvest the dividends. By beginning early and with the right attitude towards saving one will likely enjoy even greater success than we have!

And yes, you will see a steadily rising yield on your investment over the long-term. It may not be the fixed rate in my projections, but the yield will increase as time passes, likely at a higher rate than I've estimated, count on it.

Current yield as a metric

I have found most investors disagree with the Yield on Investment concept. They feel that current yield is really what's important. When you purchase a stock or reinvest the dividend, you are paying the current price, so the yield is always "Current Dividend divided by Current Price". Some even suggest that "what I get paid today matters, not future projections".

To me they are missing the point of Income investing for the future. Certainly, your current purchases determine your current yield for that purchase, but we are assuming you are investing over a long period and it's the overall yield of your total investment that determines your future growth. Current purchases are just one component of your overall yield. Your purchases may at times be higher or lower than your average yield, but dividend reinvestments and dividend increases also play an important role. It's the combination of every aspect of your income investment strategy which determines your future potential income growth.

I've shown that by following the Income investment strategy, our income and yield on investment from our TFSAs has grown over an eleven year period continuously and consistently. As we continue to invest the maximum allowed each year and reinvest our dividends, our future income and yield on investment will continue to grow, that is a given, not a guess. You want your average yield to increase over time, not just from your current purchases, reinvestments and dividend increases, but have your entire portfolio benefit from the magic of compounding.

Part of this process may best be described by the following excerpt from "Winning the Loser's Game," by Charles D. Ellis (page 124):

> *"Remember that when you buy a common stock,* ***what you really buy is the right to receive the dividends paid on that share of stock.*** *Just as we buy cows for their milk and hens for their eggs, we buy stocks for their current and future earnings and dividends. If you ran a dairy, wouldn't you prefer to have cow prices low when you were buying so you could get more gallons of milk for your investment in cows?*
>
> *The lower the price of the shares when you buy, the more shares you will get for every $1,000 you invest and* ***the greater the dollars you will receive in future dividends as a percentage of your investment (yield on investment).*** *Therefore, if you are a saver and a buyer of shares, as most investors are and will continue to be for many years, your real long-term interest is, curiously, to have*

stock prices go down quite a lot and stay down. That's why you can accumulate more shares at low prices and so receive more future dividends with the money you invest.

If you have successfully saved and invested enough to have ample funds **(income from your investments)** *for all your chosen responsibilities and obligations, you have truly won the money game. Bravo"!*

That's exactly what this book, *Your TFSA "Compounder"* is attempting to help you achieve.

Customizing the TFSA worksheets

If you would like to enter your own TFSA contributions and project your own future earnings, you can use my blank worksheets, named "Your Actual TFSA" and "Spouse Actual TFSA" (these are available as part of the "TFSA Retire 60" Excel download).

1. Enter your age in the top "Age" column and correct the ages going down the list accordingly.
2. Leave the first "Yearly Contributions" cell blank and do not change the $6,000 amounts below in this column unless Canada Revenue Agency adjusts the annual amount. If they do change the figure copy the new amount down for future years.
3. Enter the "TFSA Max Contribution" amount. This will be the maximum contribution allowed at your current age. This is particularly relevant if you have un-contributed balances from earlier years. For instance, if you turned 21 in 2020 when you started a TFSA you will be able to contribute a maximum of $23,000 (2017-2020: $5,500+$5,500+$6,000+$6,000 =$23,000, if you were 18 years old in 2017).
   *If you are 29 or older in 2020 leave it at $69,500, the maximum accumulation allowed for 2020.
4. In the first "Actual Annual Contribution" cell enter the amount you've contributed to date (this **will not** include any gains or losses, just what you've contributed to your TFSA to date). Each year after change the base of $6,000 to the amount you actually contribute.
5. The "Balance of TFSA to Contribute" and "TFSA Total Invested Value" column will calculate automatically.
6. At some date in the future the amount in the "Balance of TFSA to Contribute" will become a negative amount. You will then reduce the amount beside it in the "Annual Contribution" to bring this column to zero.

7. Enter the amount of income you earned for the current year, from your "Annual Contribution" amount, in the first cell of "Projected Income Earned each Year" column. Do not adjust the figures below on this column.
8. Your current yield in the next column will be calculated in the "Yield on Total" column.
9. Use the "Spouse Actual TFSA" worksheet (if applicable), repeating the above steps to record your spouse's contributions.

The chart below is an example of a customized chart using myself as the contributor. I started with my current age of 77 for 2019. I contributed the maximum allowed as of 2019, so under the "TFSA Max Contribution" is entered $63,500. My "Total Investment" is $77,122.04 (consisting of the $63,500 plus my reinvested dividends of $13,622.04) and under the "Income Earned each Year" column is $4,680.05, which is my income earned for 2019, and my current "Yield on Total Investment" is 6.07% ($4,680.05 / $77,122.04 x 100 = 6.07%).

HM TFSA	Yearly Contributions	TSFA Max Contributon	Annual Contribution	Balance of TFSA to Contribute	TFSA Total Invested Value	Income Earned each Year	Yield on Total Investment	Income % Inc each Year	Gth%
77		$ 63,500.00	$ 63,500.00	$ 0.00	$ 77,122.04	$ 4,680.05	6.07%		6.07%
78	$ 6,000.00	$ 69,500.00	$ 6,000.00	$ 0.00	$ 87,802.09	$ 5,549.09	6.32%	18.57%	6.32%
79	$ 6,000.00	$ 75,500.00	$ 6,000.00	$ 0.00	$ 99,351.18	$ 6,527.37	6.57%	17.63%	6.57%
80	$ 6,000.00	$ 81,500.00	$ 6,000.00	$ 0.00	$111,878.55	$ 7,630.12	6.82%	16.89%	6.82%
81	$ 6,000.00	$ 87,500.00	$ 6,000.00	$ 0.00	$125,508.67	$ 8,873.46	7.07%	16.30%	7.07%
82	$ 6,000.00	$ 93,500.00	$ 6,000.00	$ 0.00	$140,382.14	$ 10,275.97	7.32%	15.81%	7.32%
83	$ 6,000.00	$ 99,500.00	$ 6,000.00	$ 0.00	$156,658.11	$ 11,859.02	7.57%	15.41%	7.57%
84	$ 6,000.00	$105,500.00	$ 6,000.00	$ 0.00	$174,517.13	$ 13,647.24	7.82%	15.08%	7.82%
85	$ 6,000.00	$111,500.00	$ 6,000.00	$ 0.00	$194,164.37	$ 15,669.06	8.07%	14.81%	8.07%
86	$ 6,000.00	$117,500.00	$ 6,000.00	$ 0.00	$215,833.43	$ 17,957.34	8.32%	14.60%	8.32%
87	$ 6,000.00	$123,500.00	$ 6,000.00	$ 0.00	$239,790.77	$ 20,550.07	8.57%	14.44%	8.57%
88	$ 6,000.00	$129,500.00	$ 6,000.00	$ 0.00	$266,340.84	$ 23,491.26	8.82%	14.31%	8.82%
89	$ 6,000.00	$135,500.00	$ 6,000.00	$ 0.00	$295,832.10	$ 26,831.97	9.07%	14.22%	9.07%
90	$ 6,000.00	$141,500.00	$ 6,000.00	$ 0.00	$328,664.08	$ 30,631.49	9.32%	14.16%	9.32%
91	$ 6,000.00	$147,500.00	$ 6,000.00	$ 0.00	$365,295.57	$ 34,958.79	9.57%	14.13%	9.57%
92	$ 6,000.00	$153,500.00	$ 6,000.00	$ 0.00	$406,254.35	$ 39,894.18	9.82%	14.12%	9.82%

From age 78 on, I am using the same projected yield increase that I used in the "TFSA Retire 60" worksheets. In reality I expect my yield to increase at a higher rate than shown.

If you would like to enter your actual contributions each year since you started your TFSA, I have another worksheet you can use called **"Enter from 2009"**, in the **"TFSA Retire at 60"** worksheet. It may not be useful if you have withdrawn funds from your TFSA during any years since 2009. In that case stick to the first example.

You have other investments and an un-contributed TFSA balance

If you have any non-registered investments but still have an un-contributed TFSA balance, you might consider moving them to your TFSA.

1. Provided they are quality dividend growth stocks.
2. If they do not qualify as DG stocks, you may wish to sell them and use the funds to buy TFSA stocks.
3. If they qualify but you would have to claim capital gains by moving them, choose the stock(s) which have the least tax affect if moving to your TFSA.
4. Whether they are dividend growth stocks or not, if you have them transferred "In Kind" or sell the shares and transfer in the cash, you will have a capital gain or loss.
5. I cannot advise you to sell shares at a loss, but believe it will be to your advantage to get the stocks or funds into your TFSA as soon as possible.

Would you do better with an ETF

I've shown you my TFSA investment from 2009 to 2019, the income I'm generating and the rising yield over the 11 years, but what if I had just invested my money in an ETF? For a comparison let's assume I invested in XIU and reinvested the distribution each quarter and see how I would have done.

XIU	Orig Invest	Div (Inc)	% Gth	Orig + Div	Running Tot	Yield
2009	5,000	**173.88**		5173.88	5173.88	**3.36%**
2010	5,000	**288.94**	66.18%	5288.94	10462.82	**2.76%**
2011	5,000	**410.87**	42.20%	5410.87	15873.69	**2.59%**
2012	5,000	**589.00**	43.36%	5589.00	21462.69	**2.74%**
2013	5,500	**857.74**	45.63%	6357.74	27820.43	**3.08%**
2014	5,500	**957.39**	11.62%	6457.39	34277.82	**2.79%**
2015	10,000	**1395.78**	45.79%	11395.78	45673.60	**3.06%**
2016	5,500	**1211.18**	-13.23%	6711.18	52384.78	**2.31%**
2017	5,500	**1881.72**	55.36%	7381.72	59766.50	**3.15%**
2018	5,500	**2243.29**	19.21%	7743.29	67509.78	**3.32%**
2019	6,000	**2656.81**	18.43%	8656.81	76166.59	**3.49%**

Hm Tfsa	Orig Invest	Div (Inc)	% Gth	Orig + Div	Running Tot	Yield
2009	5,000	**144.94**		5,144.94	5,144.94	**2.82%**
2010	5,000	**399.00**	175.29%	5,399.00	10,543.94	**3.78%**
2011	5,000	**862.35**	116.13%	5,862.35	16,406.29	**5.26%**
2012	5,000	**959.70**	11.29%	5,959.70	22,365.99	**4.29%**
2013	5,500	**1,313.46**	36.86%	6,813.46	29,179.45	**4.50%**
2014	5,500	**1,742.35**	32.65%	7,242.35	36,421.80	**4.78%**
2015	10,000	**2,404.75**	38.02%	12,404.75	48,826.55	**4.93%**
2016	5,500	**3,301.78**	37.30%	8,801.78	57,628.33	**5.73%**
2017	5,500	**3,813.66**	15.50%	9,313.66	66,941.99	**5.70%**
2018	5,500	**4,574.95**	19.96%	10,074.95	77,016.94	**5.94%**
2019	6,000	**5,432.10**	18.74%	11,432.10	88,449.04	**6.14%**

Compare the Div (Inc) and Yield columns. Which would you rather receive?

Chapter 5

How much money do you really need to save to retire?

Here is a suggestion by Michele Cagan, CPA, an author and financial mentor, on a method to calculate how much money you should save for retirement:

> *"To come up with how much you'll need to save, start with money that's guaranteed to come in during your retirement. Subtract the expenses you realistically expect to have. The difference between those numbers is the amount your savings will need to support every month. Multiply that monthly difference by 12 (to get a year's difference) and then by 25 or 30 – the number of years you expect to spend in retirement".*

> \- Michele Cagan, CPA

Here are a few examples of her suggested calculation:

Monthly Income	$3,000	$3,100	$3,200	$3,300	$3,400
Yearly Income	$36,000	$37,200	$38,400	$39,600	$40,800
Monthly Expenses	$4,600	$4,900	$5,200	$5,500	$5,800
Yearly Expenses	$55,200	$58,800	$62,400	$66,000	$69,600
Monthly Difference	$1,600	$1,800	$2,000	$2,200	$2,400
Yearly Shortfall	$19,200	$21,600	$24,000	$26,400	$28,800
30 Years Retirement	**$576,000**	**$648,000**	**$720,000**	**$792,000**	**$864,000**

Another common suggestion I have found is that you will need a portfolio of at least a million dollars or more before you can retire comfortably. When I was still seeking "experts" for financial advice I was given this rather astronomical goal as requirement for a secure financial retirement. $1 Million is often suggested because one can expect to generate approximately $40,000 of annual income (allowing for a basic 4% interest rate: $1Million x 4.0% = $40,000). Add government pensions or other guaranteed income, say $35,000 in total, and you arrive at a potential of $75,000 of annual income before taxes.

If you're wondering how one could even amass a $1 Million dollar portfolio, consider the following projection (and wonder if it is even achievable!) Consider saving $5,000 every year for 35 years and hope to earn an annual 8.5% rate of return. If possible, here are the results:

Age	Actual Amount Invested	Market Value	Annual Return Each Year
30	$5,000.00	$5,425.00	8.50%
35	$25,000.00	$40,302.49	8.50%
40	$50,000.00	$92,746.25	8.50%
45	$75,000.00	$171,603.67	8.50%
50	$100,000.00	$290,178.15	8.50%
55	$125,000.00	$468,473.46	8.50%
60	$150,000.00	$736,568.40	8.50%
65	$175,000.00	$1,139,691.15	8.50%

The flaw with both of these scenarios is that they deal with an assumed guaranteed fixed rate of return over a long period of time. One would be wholly dependent on a consistent return, quite a high one at that, for decades at a time. Even worse, if one has a mix of fixed assets and equities, the fixed assets will provide a lower return requiring higher returns from the equities. Positive returns for 35 years from the stock market is just not possible and there are way too many variables to accurately estimate future expenses and inflation. As I showed in chapter 4 the market does not provide a positive return over 20 years, never mind 35 years.

With the stresses and increasing taxes heaped on average people and families, the ability to achieve the savings and returns to achieve those magical retirement safety nets seem a distant if not impossible goal.

The other factor is that no-one knows what your retirement expenses will be in 20 years, 30 years or longer. We've been lucky for well over a decade because inflation has been low, much lower than average. I think we could safely say that CPP and OAS will continue to represent about 40% of ones' retirement expenses. That leaves you with 60% to fund on your own, unless you are fortunate enough to have a company pension. But, let's stay with those who have no company pension, and let's not try to apply a fixed amount to save. Instead, let's look at it from a different perspective. Should future costs rise, hopefully incomes will also rise and if you save more, your rising yield on investment is what will keep your future TFSA income ahead of inflation.

But for now if $40,000 is your income goal, look at my projected TFSA chart below. The chart shows I have contributed the maximum amount each year for 11 years to 2019 ($63,500).If I continue to contribute the $6,000 each year and the income growth continues as it has over the past11 years I can expect to earn $43,997.10 of tax-free income from my TFSA account within the next 15 years. And the $43,997.10of tax-free dollars is equivalent to $57,000 before taxes.

Should the annual TFSA amount increase I would invest the higher amount and my future income would also increase, as

HM TFSA	Yearly Contributions	TFSA Max Contribution	Annual Contribution	Balance of TFSA to Contribute	TFSA Total Invested Value	Income Earned each Year	Yield on Total Investment
77		$63,500.00	$63,500.00	$0.00	$88,449.04	$5,432.10	6.14%
78	$6,000.00	$69,500.00	$6,000.00	$0.00	$99,881.14	$6,382.40	6.39%
79	$6,000.00	$75,500.00	$6,000.00	$0.00	$112,263.54	$7,454.30	6.64%
80	$6,000.00	$81,500.00	$6,000.00	$0.00	$125,717.84	$8,661.96	6.89%
81	$6,000.00	$87,500.00	$6,000.00	$0.00	$140,379.80	$10,023.12	7.14%
82	$6,000.00	$93,500.00	$6,000.00	$0.00	$156,402.92	$11,558.18	7.39%
83	$6,000.00	$99,500.00	$6,000.00	$0.00	$173,961.10	$13,290.63	7.64%
84	$6,000.00	$105,500.00	$6,000.00	$0.00	$193,251.73	$15,247.56	7.89%
85	$6,000.00	$111,500.00	$6,000.00	$0.00	$214,499.29	$17,460.24	8.14%
86	$6,000.00	$117,500.00	$6,000.00	$0.00	$237,959.53	$19,964.80	8.39%
87	$6,000.00	$123,500.00	$6,000.00	$0.00	$263,924.33	$22,803.06	8.64%
88	$6,000.00	$129,500.00	$6,000.00	$0.00	$292,727.40	$26,023.47	8.89%
89	$6,000.00	$135,500.00	$6,000.00	$0.00	$324,750.86	$29,682.23	9.14%
90	$6,000.00	$141,500.00	$6,000.00	$0.00	$360,433.09	$33,844.67	9.39%
91	$6,000.00	$147,500.00	$6,000.00	$0.00	$400,277.76	$38,586.78	9.64%
92	$6,000.00	$153,500.00	$6,000.00	$0.00	$444,864.53	$43,997.10	9.89%

would yours, keeping your future income ahead of inflation.

If at that point I no longer contribute to the TFSA but begin withdrawing the income, the $43,997.10 of income will continue to **<u>increase</u>** provided the companies continue to

raise their dividend. It is likely the annual income increase
will vary from 5% to 7% per year.

Become a big fish in a small pond

**Did you notice on my chart above, that I will only
have contributed $153,500 of my own money to
receive $43,997.10 of income from my TFSA?** My
<u>total</u> investment is $444,864.53 because of reinvested
dividends, but those dividends have and will come from the
companies I've invested in, not out of my own pocket. That's
the power of compounding!

Most assume that when you invest a lump-sum of $1 million
you could likely receive 4% on the investment, or $40,000.
Well, I'm not investing a lump-sum, instead I invested over
time, maximizing my contributions, investing in quality
dividend growth stocks and reinvested the dividends in my
TFSA. I hope I have shown you that one does not need to
accumulate $1 million to generate $40,000 of taxable annual
income upon retirement. Instead, with the magic of
compounding coupled with an Income investment strategy,
one can reach the same annual income with only
$444,864.53! In other words, I've created my own *TFSA
"Compounder"*. And, it's working as expected and so will
yours.

In 2019, my TFSA yield on my investment is 6.14% and it will
continue to rise slowly and steadily into the future, as it has
over the past 11 years. Remember, if you are reinvesting the
dividends those reinvestments will automatically generate
income and your income will compound with each
reinvestment and addition of new funds. Add any dividend
increases and this will also increase your yield, guaranteed!

The result is that I will be earning more income for every
dollar I invest as time passes. Or, you can say it in reverse; as
my yield rises it costs me less to receive one dollar of income.

We will achieve the goal of generating a retirement income because our investment strategy gives us a rising yield on our invested dollars, not a fixed or slow growing one.

So, the more important question is not how much money you need to save to retire or achieve your goal, but how much income your investments will generate to allow you to retire financially secure.

That's the big difference between Income investors and everyone else. Others look for their investments to grow in value (capital appreciation), whereas we look for our income to grow and continue to grow after retiring. Some consider it the same thing, but income growth is not affected by market movements or changes in share price. We also do not have to sell any of our investment assets for income, the money-generating pot never gets dipped into, and therefore the income stream never stops. Take a look at the income growth from my TFSA from 2009 to 2019 (on the chart below). This period includes the downturn of the financial crisis of 2008/2009 where the market prices did not recover from the 2008 highs until 2014.

Year	Maximum Contribution by Year	Dividend income by Year	Dividend % growth each Year	Original Investment plus Dividends	Accumulated investment	Yield on Investment
2009	5,000.00	144.94		5,144.94	5,144.94	2.82%
2010	5,000.00	399.00	175.29%	5,399.00	10,543.94	3.78%
2011	5,000.00	862.35	116.13%	5,862.35	16,406.29	5.26%
2012	5,000.00	959.70	11.29%	5,959.70	22,365.99	4.29%
2013	5,500.00	1313.46	36.86%	6,813.46	29,179.45	4.50%
2014	5,500.00	1742.35	32.65%	7,242.35	36,421.80	4.78%
2015	10,000.00	2404.75	38.02%	12,404.75	48,826.55	4.93%
2016	5,500.00	3301.78	37.30%	8,801.78	57,628.33	5.73%
2017	5,500.00	3813.66	15.50%	9,313.66	66,941.99	5.70%
2018	5,500.00	4574.95	19.96%	10,074.95	77,016.94	5.94%
2019	6,000.00	5432.10	18.74%	11,432.10	88,449.04	6.14%

By investing the maximum allowed in quality dividend growth stocks into my TFSA and always reinvesting the dividends during that period I was able to increase my income each and every year as well as grow the yield on my investment. Notice that the starting yield is only 2.82%.

Market value fluctuates day by day, week by week and year by year. All investors want the value of our holdings to rise and be worth more in the future, but you won't see a steady price growth as you will with your income when following the Income investment strategy. It's not the size of the pile (your investments), but the income you receive from what you invest that will guarantee a worry-free retirement.

What's more, by investing for income you'll see your income grow, slowly reaching a point where the income meets your expense needs and that's when you can relax and begin to feel you've accomplished your investment goal.

It gets better because your growing income doesn't stop, rather, it continues to grow because your quality dividend growth stocks will continue to raise their dividends, so your retirement income grows faster than inflation.And never forget that when this investment is within a TFSA, it is tax-free!

Inflation: up, up and up!

> *Inflation is a rise in the general level of prices of goods and services in an economy over a period of time. When the general price level rises, each unit of currency buys fewer goods and services. Consequently, inflation also reflects an erosion in the purchasing power of money – a loss of real value in the internal medium of exchange and unit of account in the economy. A chief measure of price inflation is the inflation rate, the annualized percentage change in a general price index normally the Consumer Price Index over time.*

You cannot plan for the future and overlook the hidden cost of inflation. The problem is that cash and fixed assets *depreciate* in value over time. We know that what costs $10 today could cost $20, $40, even $100 in the future. We can make some assumptions based on the past, but for the past decade we've lived with extremely low inflation (1% - 1.5%) and it would be too easy to believe it will remain that low. The average inflation rate since 1918 has been 2.9% per year, meaning prices double every 25 years. Should normal inflation rates return, they will significantly increase our future expenses!

I must admit that I have always questioned those inflation percentages. To me it seems that many essential items have increased in price much faster than the reported inflation rates.

In the Lee Child novels his character, Jack Reacher, often says, *"Hope for the best, but plan for the worst"*.

I believe it is prudent to apply that rule to inflation: hope that inflation remains low or below average, but plan for much higher inflation and costs in the future.

How much income do you need?

You can never have enough, if you ask me. There are four areas of concern which can affect every retirees income:

1. Company crisis

I read an article in the Financial Post, August 22, 2019 by Tom Bradley, here's a quote:

> "What do the bad outcomes look like? *Assume your stocks drop 25 per cent. What does this translate into in dollar terms? How does it feel to lose **$250,000** on a million-dollar portfolio? And how will it feel if your income drops because a couple of holdings cut their dividends*"?

Dividend cuts are a possibility, even from companies which have paid and raised them for many years. It has happened in the past and I'm sure it will happen to other quality companies in the future. Dividend cuts by some stocks you own don't necessarily mean your overall income will drop. But those who invest for capital appreciation can't say the same about price drops. How long would it take to recover from a $250,000 drop in value? Some might never gain it back, especially if the market continued to drop and stayed down for a while.

2. Inflation

Inflation has been discussed, but too often over-looked. Should the economy turn for the worst, high inflation rates, like those experienced in the 1970s, may occur and often the increases happen quickly.

3. Life Changes

We all hope that as we age we have the opportunity to relax and enjoy our retirement years in general good health, but possible illness and physical impairment may require extensive care, possibly moving to a care facility or one might wish to use in-home care. All are expensive and they are not fixed costs.

4. Family Changes

Ideally, we would like to believe that ones' family will be there to assist should help or support be needed, but too often the reverse is the case. Families become busy, move or there may even be a parting of the ways. Those of us who have the benefit of family support, when needed, should be extremely grateful.

We can't foresee the future and we know things can and will change, so the more income your investments generate the safer you and your financial status will be. Just keep to the same path and count on your ever-growing income from your *TFSA "Compounder"*.

The Exit Plan

As with the start of our journey, you should prepare a plan for the end. The exit plan and disbursement of your estate is YOUR decision, no one else's. Make it easy by preparing and updating the following documents as situations change.

1. **A Personal Directive**
   Allows you to name the person(s) you trust to make decisions on your behalf should you lose mental capacity and lists the areas in which they have decision-making authority.
2. **An Enduring Power of Attorney**
   An agreement between you and a person you trust that allows them to make financial decisions on your behalf if you're no longer capable of making these decisions.
3. **A Will**
   A legal document by which you assign an executor to carry out your wishes as to how your property is to be distributed at death. Be specific and don't be influenced by others.

4. **Assign "Successor Holder" to your TFSA**
The surviving spouse or common-law-partner can roll over a TFSA into their TFSA tax exempt. Here's a more detailed description excerpted from Canada Revenue Agency:

"Designation of an exempt contribution by a survivor":

If designated as a beneficiary, the survivor has the option to contribute and designate all or a portion of a survivor payment as an exempt contribution to their own TFSA, without affecting their own unused TFSA contribution room, subject to certain conditions and limits.

Beneficiaries (other than the survivor) who receive a payment from the deceased holder's TFSA, cannot contribute and designate any amount as an exempt contribution.

For the survivor to designate an exempt contribution, the amount must be received and contributed to their TFSA during the rollover period (end of the calendar year end). Also, the survivor must designate their survivor payments as an exempt contribution on Form RC240, Designation of an Exempt Contribution Tax-Free Savings Account (TFSA), and send the designation within 30 days after the day the contribution is made or at a later time as permitted by the specified Minister.

The total exempt contributions designated during the rollover period cannot exceed the fair market value of the deceased holder's TFSA at the time of death.

What's the withdrawal plan in the future?

When you're ready to retire here's how I suggest you withdraw funds to cover your retirement expenses:

1. Draw down your RRSP money first to meet your living expenses as they will be taxed at the highest rate.
2. If you have a company pension you may wish to defer it and allow it to continue to grow.
3. Continue contributing the maximum allowable amount to your TFSA.
4. Defer applying for CPP and OAS till age 70. You will get 8.4% more CPP for every year after age 65 and 7.2% more OAS for every year after age 65.
5. When your RRSP is nearly depleted begin drawing your company pension (if available) or CPP and OAS.
6. If you still need funds to cover expenses begin to withdraw TFSA funds as needed.
7. Since **TFSA** withdrawals aren't taxable, they won't be added to your income. They **can**'t **affect** your **eligibility** for federal benefits and credits based on income, such as the Working Income Tax Benefit (WITB), the Guaranteed Income Supplement (**GIS**) or the Goods and Services Tax credit.
8. The retired may even qualify for the Guaranteed Income Supplement (GIS), especially if your only taxable income is CPP and OAS.
9. That's it, your home free. And tax-free! (Or should I say as tax-free as can be!)

The goal of this book is to have your TFSA generate as much tax-free income as possible. If you have taxable income sources draw it (them) down first and then finally your TFSA funds. Each persons' financial situation will vary and you should do your own assessment to determine the withdrawal plan that suits your particular needs. However, if you have followed the *TFSA "Compounder"* strategy, I'm sure it will simplify your decision.

Don't change your investment strategy in retirement

As one gets closer to retirement, you will often hear recommendations to change your current investment strategy by increasing the fixed asset allocation.

> *"You almost certainly want exposure to bonds in your portfolio, with your exact weighting tied to your age, risk tolerance, investing goals and such"* -"How not to move back in with your parents: the young person's complete guide to financial empowerment" by Rob Carrick.

Of course, these recommendations relate to protecting the value of your portfolio should the market drop. However, if you've followed the Income investment strategy and your income has grown and continues to grow over the years, why would every consider switching to a fixed income?

If my wife and I were to follow such advice we'd be sitting with 78% bonds or other fixed assets and most likely giving up the larger portion of our growing income each year (which was up over 10% for 2018 and 2019) for a fixed income? Thanks, but no thanks!

Instead, I suggest that you stick to your dividend growth stocks in your TFSA and other investments in retirement, as we do. Just sit back and continue collecting those ever-rising dividends and a higher income each year.

Oh, did I mention one of the biggest advantages of this strategy? You'll look forward with joyful anticipation to receiving your dividend payment, and the joy you feel only increases as your dividends increase!

So what really makes the *TFSA "Compounder"* strategy work?

Here's the most important takeaway from my entire investing philosophy, ***if you invest in quality dividend growth stocks to generate an income, the companies also contribute by paying you a dividend. You will reinvest the dividends to buy more shares and increase your income. Finally, when the companies raise the dividend on all the shares you own it will further grow your income. You should continue to add funds and the process accelerates. In other words, the companies are helping you to grow your income by adding to what you contribute, so you don't need to save as much to reach your income goal!***

That's how and why the yield on your *TFSA "Compounder"* and investments rises. In addition, because we are concentrating the majority of our investments into a TFSA, every dollar we put into it and every dollar of growth is tax-free. Plus, the sooner you reach your allowable contribution maximum the greater the growth.

No one will have their hand out, looking to collect their share. It's all yours with no strings attached.

I cannot stress enough the concept of the **Rising Yield**, because it's the key to earning enough income to retire without having to depend upon selling your capital or needing to invest larger sums to obtain the same results.

Those who invest for capital appreciation (the price rising) need and hope their stock prices go up continuously, which is a risky endeavor. Any drop in market value requires a greater increase to recover. A 20% drop in your portfolio value requires a 25% gain, a 35% drop needs about a 54% gain and a 50% drop requires a 100% increase to get back to the original value.

No one wants to be a slave to the temperamental market, nervously watching price. Through the use of my investment strategy I have not had to worry about market performance for over a decade.

To me, it's such a simple concept that I wonder why so few recognize it. ***The longer you hold shares of solid dividend growth stocks, the greater your income and yield will become***.

That's the point I am trying to get across with my book, if you invest regularly, reinvest the dividends, continue to buy more shares (the lower the price the better) and receive regular dividend increases, then there is no reason not to expect to retire with a steadily growing income from your TFSA. When you track your income progress (which will be discussed in Chapter 6) you will know long before you retire just how well you're doing. Imagine, seeing your income grow each month or quarter, slowly getting closer and closer towards your goal. And if you're like me, you will gain a lot of comfort knowing your future is on its way to being financially secure.

Although I am advocating a singular form of investing, one that seems counterintuitive to most popular forms of portfolio building, I am very confident that you can and will benefit from it in ways that other forms of investing cannot provide. Income investing does require patience, it's a long-haul form of income growth, but in the end, aren't we all looking for the same end goal? To have enough money to see us through retirement in financial security and comfort!

Following the Income investment strategy within your TFSA is a sure way to generate an ever-growing income for your retirement. But remember, we are always seeking a reasonable yield on our purchases, so don't get side-tracked by trying to rush or speed things up by chasing higher yields. You'll regret it and at some point recognize your mistake, likely when the dividend is cut.

If financial freedom in retirement is important to you, than I believe very strongly that if you set your own income goal, work to make saving a priority and follow the *TFSA "Compounder"* investment strategy, you will make it to the finish line a winner.

The TFSA Compounding machine

I have tried to demonstrate throughout this book that by combining the Income investment strategy with a TFSA account, you can create your own *TFSA "Compounder"* or compounding machine. Rather than repeat myself or try to say it more eloquently, I think others have expressed it better.

*"The **compounding machine** stocks are the Holy grail of investment."* - Mohnish Pabrai

*"To his son, [Shelby] Davis passed along his infectious passion for owning shares in carefully chosen companies (he called them "**compounding machines'**), his conviction that owning the **best compounding machines** would lead to unimagined rewards, his distrust of unnecessary spending (why waste money they could be invested?), and his workaholic tendencies."*
-The DavisDynasty

*"What we learned is that if you buy a good and sustainable business, then over time the return of that business will do the natural **compounding** for you."* - William Browne

*"**Compounders** are generally market leaders, with high barriers to entry and high returns on capital, whose intrinsic values are growing at a healthy rate. The reason they can be mispriced is typically a function of time horizon. When investor's don't focus on the distant **compounding** merit of a great business, they may not assign that merit a fair value."* -Christopher Begg

*"Our strategy is to own high quality, modestly valued business over many years, to take advantage of the power of **compounding** as earnings grow. To do*

*that successfully only works if we avoid mistakes –
unforced errors – that interrupt the power of*
compounding.*"* - Ira Rothberg

*"If you're going to own a company for a long time,
the earnings it generates today will be a small
component of the eventual return. Much more
important will be how those earnings can be
reinvested over time to build value. When companies
with positive* **compounding characteristics**
*become available at really attractive prices, we'll
hope to take advantage."* - Chris Davis

"What I have learnt is don't sell the **compounders**
*when they get fully priced or they get over-priced.
Only sell the compounders when it's absolutely
obvious to you that it isn't egregiously priced. The big
money is in riding the* **compounders** *but you have
to try to get in at a reasonable valuation and you
have to be right on the fact they are* **compounders**.
*It's a forgiving business, so you can be wrong quite a
few times and still be ok. It was a difficult lesson for a
cheapskate for me. It was a very difficult lesson for
Warren and Charlie. I think they learnt the lesson
from See's Candy, that was a seminal lesson for
them."* –Mohnish Pabrai

*"Some of our biggest mistakes have been in selling
down positions in great businesses when we thought
they were fairly valued, or even a bit overvalued. In
our experience,* **compounders** *tend to keep
compounding, so we're slow to sell unless something
in the business or company has fundamentally
changed or if the valuation has just become extreme."*
- Peter Keefe

Chapter 6

The Five & Ten-Stock Income Growth portfolio

The Five-Stock Income portfolio:

This strategy is suitable for a beginner, a child's portfolio (could be in an adult's name), or even for one who is just looking for a simplified income growth portfolio.

Guidelines: Select one stock from each of the five categories:

> Bank
> Utility
> Communications
> Pipeline
> Low yield/high growth

How to invest:

It is recommended that you have an investment account with Wealthsimple Trade.

The first choice would be a TFSA account, secondly a Non-registered account.

Try to set up a specific monthly amount to invest ($50, $75, $100, or more).

Buy Fractional shares of the five stocks, in equal dollar amounts with your monthly contribution.

Set up automatic dividend reinvestment for the account.

Record the stock purchases and dividend reinvestments in the Excel worksheet.

When you can afford to, increase the monthly contributions.

There is no need to rebalance the holdings, or consider adding any other stocks.

Do not sell any of the stocks, unless one of the companies cuts the dividend.

If you did sell a stock, select a new stock in the same category, and use the funds to buy shares in the new stock.

With the Five-Stock portfolio, you will be investing on a regular basis, hopefully monthly, and applying the dollar cost averaging (not worrying about the current price).

The Ten-Stock Advanced Income portfolio:

Guidelines: Select two stocks from each of the five categories:

> Bank
> Utility
> Communications
> Pipeline
> Low yield/high growth

How to invest:

It is recommended that you have an investment account with Wealthsimple Trade.

The first choice would be a TFSA account, secondly a Non-registered account.

Set up the Yield Difference worksheet with the ten stocks listed by category, or sector.

Always buy Fractional shares.

When you have money to invest ($100, $500, $1,000 or more), enter the current price of each ten stocks into the Yield difference worksheet, and buy an equal amount of the stock in each category, with the highest yield difference.

Set up automatic dividend reinvestment for the account.

Record the stock purchases and dividend reinvestments in the Excel worksheet.

There is no need to rebalance the holdings, however, you can consider adding other quality stocks from a different sector.

If you do add new stocks, continue spreading your new investments equally between the stocks in each sector.

Do not sell any of the stocks, unless one of the companies cuts the dividend.

If you did sell a stock, select a new stock in the same category, and use the funds to buy shares in the new stock.

With the Ten-Stock portfolio, you are looking to buy stocks which offer a slightly higher yield, and you can decide when to invest (looking to buy during a market dip), or ignore current market price, and invest on a regular basis.

Select your stocks following the four-rule test described in this book. Make your evaluation and selection from the list of 45 Canadian dividend growth stocks, listed in my book *Income Investing Explained*, or the 29 Average Yield/Average Growth, and 13 Low Yield/High Growth listed in *Salary for Life*.

Monitoring your portfolio

How should the income investor monitor their TFSA portfolio? Well, you definitely want to avoid using "**Stop-Losses**". Stop-losses are where one would set a sell price should the price of a stock drop to a certain set price. This may be a viable method for those investing for growth or buying and selling shares, but should never be used by Income growth investors. Our intention is to hold your dividend growth stocks as long as they continue to pay and raise their dividend.

For Income investors, the dividend income and the income growth are what we watch. Most quality dividend growth companies have a regular dividend payment routine. Each quarter the board of directors announces the dividend to be paid the next quarter. However, those that raise their dividend they usually do it the same quarter each year. Most Canadian banks raise their dividend twice a year.

Knowing when companies pay and raise their dividend is the key. As long as they meet these pay dates and raise their dividend as expected, you can be assured that the company is in good shape. You don't need to scour the financial statements or listen to expert opinions. The dividends should be so regular and consistent that you could set your calendar by their confirmation.

Making it easy to monitor an income portfolio:

Keeping track of the dividend growth percentage from one year to the next year and the rising yield on your total investments are one of the most important aspects of monitoring your holdings.

The next section covers how to record your investment transactions. One of the more unrecognized advantages of monitoring your portfolio is the thrill of seeing your TFSA income grow. Every time your dividend payment is deposited in your account and reinvested, you record it in your worksheets. I have never tired of reviewing my records and I have never lost the pleasure of having my investing decisions confirmed quarter after quarter. I hope you will enjoy this part of the process as much as I have!

Recording your investments

I'm not referring to tracking the price of your holdings or how much your investments are worth. You can, if you wish, but what you really want to monitor is your income and the income growth.

In order to really appreciate income investing you must track the income your stocks are producing. It's not going to be sudden jumps upward, but a slow and gradual increase over time.

```
SHAREOWNER STOCKS:
HENRY'S\TFSA SHAREOWNER CASH
HENRY'S\TFSA SHAREOWNER STKS
  SUB-TOTAL HM TFSA

HENRY RRIF SHAREOWNER CASH
HM STOCKS VALUE
  SUB-TOTAL HM STOCKS

RAE'S RRIF SHAREOWNER CASH
RAE'S RRSP SHAREHOLDER STOCKS
  SUB-TOTAL RM RRSP

JOINT SHAREOWNER CASH
JOINT STOCKS VALUE

  TOTAL JOINT STOCKS

RAE'S\TFSA SHAREOWNER CASH
RAE'S\TFSA SHAREOWNER STKS
  SUB-TOTAL RM TFSA
```

I use an accounting program (which is not mandatory) because I was an accountant and like to account for all the pennies on all our transactions.

This screen shows how our accounts are setup. There is a "Cash" and "Stk" line for each account (TFSA, RRIF, Joint, etc.).

In the "Cash" account line, most transactions including commissions are coded to the matching stock account (TFSA cash entries are coded to TFSA stocks, and so on). The only transactions coded elsewhere are the account fees that are not related to stock purchases/sales. The sub-total accounts are my total investment in each category. I then use an Excel worksheet with several sub-worksheets where I re-enter the same transactions (discussed next), which provides the specific details on each stock and includes many more reports to record and track the income and summarize my holdings.

Recording stock transactions in Excel

I have setup a complete Excel worksheet to record all your stock transactions. You would download the "Sample Cdn Reports New" Excel worksheet from:

https://drive.google.com/drive/u/1/folders/1kD-ZtK7WkIINobzB3HYJ1tnwnh9P3NDf

The "Sample Cdn Reports New" worksheet includes:

- Summary Report
- TFSA: Stock Transaction worksheet -10 stocks
- RRSP: Stock Transaction worksheet - 10 stocks
- Non-Reg: Stock Transaction worksheet-10 stocks
- DRIP: Stock Transaction worksheet -5 stocks
- Activity Report for Non-Reg, RRSP, TFSA & DRIP
- Yield Projection
- Dividend Growth (Div Gth) Calculation
- Average Yield (%GthYld) Calculation
- TSX 60 Listing & Exercise sheet
- NOBL Listing & Exercise sheet

There is a separate Excel worksheet with the TFSA projections, called "TFSA Retire at 60", which can be downloaded from the same location.

Here is a sample of an individual stock transaction entry worksheet:

Sample Stock 1

Settlement Date	Action	Number of Shares	Price Per Share	Comm Fee	Number of Share Bal	ACB (Investment)	ACB per Share	Capital Gain (Loss)	Dividend Shares
3-Mar	Buy	100	$50.00	$10	100	$5,010.00	$50.10	–	0.00
1-May	Sell	-50	$120.00	$10	50	$2,505.00	$50.10	3,485.00	0.00
18-Jul	Buy	50	$130.00	$10	100	$9,015.00	$90.15	0.00	0.00
25-Sep	Sell	-40	$90.00	$10	60	$5,409.00	$90.15	-16.00	0.00
26-Sep	Div	1	$98.00	$0	61	$5,507.00	$90.28	0.00	1.00
27-Sep	Div	1	$120.00	$0	62	$5,627.00	$90.76	0.00	1.00
					62	$5,627.00	$90.76	0.00	0.00
				Totals	62	$5,627.00	$90.76		2.00

Record your Buys, Sells and the Dividend Reinvestments, for each stock on a similar worksheet. I've separated the stocks by accounts, TFSA, RRSP/RRIF, Non-Registered and even DRIP accounts. I've allowed for 10 stocks in each category. You add additional one, but you'll have to add them to the Summary report, in the right section and adjust the formulas.

Here's part of a Summary Report (a sample):

						Portfolio Summary Report			
TFSA Stocks	Adj Cost Base	ADC Per Share	Dividend Shares	Bought Shares	Number of Shares	DIV	Yearly Div	Ave Yield	Qt
1st	$5,627.00	$90.76	$2.00	$60.00	62.0000	3.60	$223.20	3.97%	
2nd	#DIV/0!	#DIV/0!	0.0000	$0.00	0.0000	1.00	$0.00	#DIV/0!	
3rd	#DIV/0!	#DIV/0!	0.0000	$0.00	0.0000	1.00	$0.00	#DIV/0!	
4th	#DIV/0!	#DIV/0!	0.0000	$0.00	0.0000	1.00	$0.00	#DIV/0!	
5th	#DIV/0!	#DIV/0!	0.0000	$0.00	0.0000	1.00	$0.00	#DIV/0!	
6th	#DIV/0!	#DIV/0!	0.0000	$0.00	0.0000	1.00	$0.00	#DIV/0!	
7th	#DIV/0!	#DIV/0!	0.0000	$0.00	0.0000	1.00	$0.00	#DIV/0!	
8th	#DIV/0!	#DIV/0!	0.0000	$0.00	0.0000	1.00	$0.00	#DIV/0!	
9th	#DIV/0!	#DIV/0!	0.0000	$0.00	0.0000	1.00	$0.00	#DIV/0!	
10th	#DIV/0!	#DIV/0!	0.0000	$0.00	0.0000	1.00	$0.00	#DIV/0!	
Total TFSA	#DIV/0!		2.0000	60.0000	62.0000		$223.20	#DIV/0!	
Un-Invested	$0.00								

Look at the "1st" line and see that the figures match the Transaction totals above.

When the annual dividend paid by the "**Div**"

"Number of Shares" column MUST match with the number of shares in your broker account for each stock. If out, check your individual stock entries.

Notice the tabs at the bottom. The RRSP and TFSA are the other sub-worksheets which is where you actually record the transactions.

These two reports, Transaction and Summary, are the key reports in my Excel worksheets. You can design many other worksheets to provide specific information to track your own stocks or use them to provide the information that's important to you. I cannot express how handy I find Excel for tracking my investments. However, if you are not as familiar with Excel, I hope you can learn to use it, even if you only have a very elementary understanding of a basic worksheet. (Or, perhaps you could have a friend, or your kids or even your grandkids help you out). You may have your own method of recording, so my explanation is brief. Here is reminder that you can download samples of my Excel worksheets to help you get started:

You can Download my "Cdn Stock ACB Report Summary" Excel worksheet at:

https://drive.google.com/drive/u/1/folders/1kD-ZtK7WkIINobzB3HYJ1tnwnh9P3NDf

The sample worksheet includes:

- Summary Report
- TFSA: Stock Transaction worksheet - 10 stocks
- RRSP: Stock Transaction worksheet - 10 stocks
- Non-Reg: Stock Transaction worksheet- 10 stocks
- DRIP: Stock Transaction worksheet - 10 stocks
- Yield Projection
- Dividend Growth (DivGth) Calculation
- 10-Yr Average Yield (%Gth Yld) Calculation
- TSX 60 Listing & Exercise sheet
- NOBL Listing & Exercise sheet
- ACB Sample
- And others

NOTE:
1. The Adjusted Cost Base (ACB) for each stock will be calculated with each transaction.
2. The ACB per share is also show.
3. Capital Gains or Losses are shown when all or a portion of your stocks are sold.
4. Remember to update the annual dividend paid, when a company increases or cuts their dividend.
5. Save your worksheet every time you make entries.
6. Save the worksheet, under a different name at the end of each month, or for sure at the end of each year.

I promise that once you've used Excel for a while making the entries will become easy and fast. I probably spend less than 20 minutes a week making entries, but spend more time watching the changes each entry has on my total income. Some would say watching paint dry is faster, but I argue, it's definitely not as satisfying!

TFSA Retire at 60 worksheet includes:
- TFSA allowable contributions since 2009
- Projection worksheets for starting ages 18, 25, 30, 40, 45
- Worksheets to record you and your spouse (if applicable) actual TFSAs contributions.
- And some miscellaneous worksheets.

You can download a set of my "Sample Cdn Reports New" as well as the "TFSA Retire at 60"at:

https://drive.google.com/drive/u/1/folders/1kD-ZtK7WkIINobzB3HYJ1tnwnh9P3NDf

BACKUP the data, often and on different sources.

We've just completed a review of the recording process of your stock transactions, but imagine if you had months or even years of transactions entered and suddenly you lost all access to all that information. How would you ever recover the information? You wouldn't, rather you'd probably have to start with the balances as of that date and carry forward.

Backup devices can be as simple as a small memory stick or a larger hard drive, by larger I mean storage capacity, not the physical size.

I personally recommend you always have two copies of all your important files. That's two backup copies, not just one on your computer and the other on a storage device. Have two separate storage devices and alternate between them when doing backups. You should backup at least one a week, more often if you are recording a lot of information or have done major changes to any of your computer work, which could be on other programs.

When saving your stock Excel worksheets I also recommend changing the name of the file, especially at year-end. For example, if your file is currently called "2019 TFSA Worksheet", once you've completed all December transactions save the file as "2019_12 TFSA Worksheet". Then immediately re-save the file as "2020 TFSA Worksheet". Now you are ready to begin recording 2020 transactions in a new file.

I save a copy of my worksheet every month, giving it a new name from my on-going worksheet. So, if I did accidently delete my current worksheet, at worst I'd only have to enter one month of transactions.

Final Comments

I'd like to take the opportunity to provide a list of lessons I've learned and important points to remember if you're seriously interested in starting this TFSA journey with Income growth investing:

- Consider your TFSA contributions as a long-term investment, not a savings account to be drawn upon.
- If a company does not pay a dividend, avoid, otherwise you are completely dependent on the price rising and your only return is when/if you sell the stock.
- It's not just which dividend stock, but which **dividend growth** stock to buy. Be conscious of what to buy and when. When stock prices go down, your stock purchases rise, and you will generate more TFSA retirement income.
- Being widely diversified is not the answer, instead concentrate on holding a few quality dividend growth stocks from a few sectors in your TFSA.
- Dividend growth is about future earnings of your TFSA, not current earnings.
- Dividend growth year after year will lead you to finding high quality stocks (ones which have rising earnings year after year).
- Reinvesting dividends and being able to purchase fractions of shares greatly enhances compounding.
- In the long-term, dividend growth encourages the price of the stock to grow.
- Let dividend yield and yield on investment, be your benchmark, not whether your portfolio beats the market index.

APPENDIX A

TSX 60 Stocks

	Symbol	Company	Sector
1	AEM	Agnico Eagle Mines Limited	Materials
2	ATD.B	Alimentation Couche-Tard Inc.	Consumer Staples
3	ARX	ARC Resources Ltd.	Energy
4	BMO	Bank of Montreal	Financials
5	BNS	Bank of Nova Scotia	Financials
6	ABX	Barrick Gold Corporation	Materials
7	BHC	Bausch Health Companies Inc.	Health Care
8	BCE	BCE Inc.	Telecommunication
9	BB	BlackBerry Limited	Information Tech
10	BBD.B	Bombardier Inc.	Industrials
11	BAM.A	Brookfield Asset Management Inc.	Financials
12	CCO	Cameco Corporation	Energy
13	CM	Canadian Imperial Bank of Commerce	Financials
14	CNR	Canadian National Railway Company	Industrials
15	CNQ	Canadian Natural Resources Limited	Energy
16	CP	Canadian Pacific Railway Limited	Industrials
17	CTC.A	Canadian Tire Corporation, Limited	Consumer Disc
18	CCL.B	CCL Industries Inc.	Materials

19	CVE	Cenovus Energy Inc.	Energy
20	GIB.A	CGI Group Inc.	Information Tech
21	CSU	Constellation Software Inc.	Information Tech
22	CPG	Crescent Point Energy Corp.	Energy
23	DOL	Dollarama Inc.	Consumer Disc
24	EMA	Emera Incorporated	Utilities
25	ENB	Enbridge Inc.	Energy
26	ECA	Encana Corporation	Energy
27	FM	First Quantum Minerals Ltd.	Materials
28	FTS	Fortis Inc.	Utilities
29	FNV	Franco-Nevada Corporation	Materials
30	WN	George Weston Limited	Consumer Staples
31	GIL	Gildan Activewear Inc.	Consumer Disc
32	G	Goldcorp Inc.	Materials
33	HSE	Husky Energy Inc.	Energy
34	IMO	Imperial Oil Limited	Energy
35	IPL	Inter Pipeline Ltd.	Energy
36	K	Kinross Gold Corporation	Materials
37	L	Loblaw Companies Limited	Consumer Staples
38	MG	Magna International Inc.	Consumer Disc
39	MFC	Manulife Financial Corporation	Financials
40	MRU	Metro Inc.	Consumer Staples

41	NA	National Bank of Canada	Financials
42	NTR	Nutrien Inc.	Materials
43	OTEX	Open Text Corporation	Information Tech
44	PPL	Pembina Pipeline Corporation	Energy
45	POW	Power Corporation of Canada	Financials
46	QSR	Restaurant Brands International Inc	Consumer Disc
47	RCI.B	Rogers Communications Inc.	Telecom
48	RY	Royal Bank of Canada	Financials
49	SAP	Saputo Inc.	Consumer Staples
50	SJR.B	Shaw Communications Inc.	Telecom
51	SNC	SNC-Lavalin Group Inc.	Industrials
52	SLF	Sun Life Financial Inc.	Financials
53	SU	Suncor Energy Inc.	Energy
54	TECK.B	Teck Resources Limited	Materials
55	T	Telus Corporation	Telecom
56	TRI	Thomson Reuters Corporation	Consumer Disc
57	TD	Toronto-Dominion Bank	Financials
58	TRP	TransCanada Corporation	Energy
59	WCN	Waste Connections US Inc.	Industrials
60	WPM	Wheaton Precious Metals Corp	Materials

APPENDIX B

Web sites recommended

Morningstar home page:
https://www.morningstar.ca/ca/membership/FeatureMatrix.aspx#334-hidenews

The Dividend Channel:
https://www.dividendchannel.com/history/?symbol=xiu.ca

Yahoo Finance:
https://ca.finance.yahoo.com/quote/ENB.TO/history?ltr=1

**Dividend Growth Investing &
Retirement:**https://www.dividendgrowthinvestingandretirement.com/canadian-dividend-all-star-list/

ca.DividendInvestor.com
http://ca.dividendinvestor.com/

**Canada Revenue Agency guidelines for the
TFSA:**https://www.canada.ca/en/revenue-agency/services/forms-publications/publications/rc4466/tax-free-savings-account-tfsa-guide-individuals.html

My Own Advisor:
https://www.myownadvisor.ca/

Adjusted Cost Base:
https://www.adjustedcostbase.ca/

My Other Books:

This book introduced the Income Growth Investment Strategy, and outlines a different approach to investing than trying to Beat the Market. It provides a detailed evaluation process and an easy-to-follow method for financial success.

This is the US edition, which concentrates on US stocks for those who want to follow the Income Growth Investment Strategy in the American market.

Income Investing Explained, addresses the investment decisions one needs to make after they have created their "List of Stocks to Consider". Which stocks to buy, when to buy, when to consider selling and how market conditions might change those decisions?

About the author

My wife Raelene and I are retired and we are both in our late 70s. I am also the author of *Your Ever Growing Income, the Rising Yield on Investments*. It is the strategy we are applying directly to investing in a TFSA.

We were retired before the TFSA was introduced in 2009, but we still managed to achieve what I consider financial freedom by following the Income Investment strategy. I wish that we could have had the opportunity to follow the process outlined in this book right from the beginning, as it is, we are now faced with high taxes on our RRIF withdrawals. But I hope you will find the proposed TFSA approach helpful and seriously contemplate adopting this investment strategy.

Like many we do not have a company pension and had to save for our retirement and find a way for our saving to supplement our CPP and OAS pensions. Thankfully we discovered Income investing and now want to pass along what we have learned. Living off your income is possible even for the average person, one just needs set their goal and work towards it.

I hope that you have enjoyed learning about this TFSA investment strategy, and I would appreciate any comments or feedback, feel free to provide them on Amazon. I wish you all the best with your own investment journey. If you would like to contact me directly email me at:

HMyourgrowingincome@gmail.com

Join me at my blog:
https://risingyieldoninvestments.blogspot.com/

Make a Donation and Get some help

If you have read this or any of my other books, and decide that Income investing is for you, but feel you could use some hands-on assistance, I may be able to help.

I'm offering a unique coaching service, where I'll provide some assistance, but instead of paying me for my help, you'll make a Donation to the Salvation Army. I have no association with the Salvation Army, and for any donations you make, you will receive a tax donation receipt.

How we might help:

1. Provide some coaching about Income Investing.
2. Provide an opinion about your portfolio.
3. Help with learning how to gather and use data to evaluate stocks.
4. Deciding which stocks and when to consider buying.

Here is how the service will work:

1. You will send me an email, at: Incomeinvesting101@gmail.com, requesting assistance.

2. I will either answer your question or specify what the
    fee will be.
3. If you agree to the fee, you will make a donation to the
    Salvation Army.
4. Provide me a copy of the donation (Do Not include
    any credit card information).
5. I will then provide what assistance I can, or answer
    your specific questions.
6. If you have further questions regarding my response
    or have additional questions on the same matter there
    will be no further fees assessed.

*Any and all information you provide will be confidential
and will not be used or referred to in any way, unless you
provide prior approval.*

*Any advice or suggestions made by me, must not be
considered financial advice. They are opinions, suggestions,
and my assessment of the requests made. It up to you to
decide how to use any suggestions, and the final decision
will always be yours to act upon them, or not.*

Made in the USA
Monee, IL
25 November 2023

47333103R00096